UNIQUE EATS AND EATERIES

OF

OMAHA

Reedy Press
PO Box 5131
St. Louis, MO 63139
www.reedypress.com

Library of Congress Control Number: 2018962615
ISBN: 9781681062075

Book Design: Barbara Northcott

Printed in the United States of America
19 20 21 22 23   5 4 3 2 1

UNIQUE EATS AND EATERIES

OF

OMAHA

TIM AND LISA TRUDELL

DEDICATION

This book is dedicated to the great chefs in our families. From grandmas, fathers, and mothers to sisters, brothers, and daughters, we have been blessed to know wonderful cooks.

CONTENTS

INTRODUCTION

Sharing Omaha with thousands of others with our first book, *100 Things to Do in Omaha Before You Die*, whetted our appetite for more opportunities to shine the spotlight on the Big O. Omaha is considered an up-and-coming foodie city OR one of the best cities in the country for foodies. It all depends on whom you follow. Regardless, the city is home to so many impressive restaurants, chefs, and culinary styles.

From authentic Italian dishes to the best steak you'll ever taste to great burgers, Omaha has something for everyone. In discussing the book with a friend, she mentioned that our city is fortunate to have so much diversity when it comes to food. Other than Antarctica, it's possible to find a food style from every continent. Omaha's food scene stretches across the city into the suburbs. You can try a local eatery each day of the year and be hard-pressed to run out of new and exciting places to eat.

In talking with chefs and restaurant owners in creating *Unique Eats and Eateries of Omaha*, we were impressed with the true love each feels for not only their eatery but also for the Omaha Metro area. People love the city and love doing their part to share it with the world. Their passion for their craft comes through with their dishes. From The Grey Plume's dedication to being ecologically responsible to Dante's commitment to working with local farmers in providing locally sourced ingredients, restaurant owners' commitment to social responsibility is laudable.

The restaurants in this book resemble ones we look for when we travel. While chain restaurants are important, we enjoy finding local cafés, restaurants, coffee shops, and dessert spots when we travel to new cities. It helps tell a community's story. We love classic restaurants. That's the same philosophy we followed in creating this book.

This book is the story about our love for Omaha. In sharing the ninety eatery-related stories, we look at family-owned restaurants, some of which have been in the family for nearly a century. Others are infants when compared with a restaurant such as Johnny's Café, which opened its doors in 1922. As fans of classic restaurants, you won't find many new eateries in the book. You will find stories of people who—as we discerned during our conversations—had the restaurant life in their blood. Some worked for such outlets as Orsi's Bakery as young children around eight years old. They grew up to have their own establishments. Some restaurateurs are third- or fourth-generation members to run their places.

The first thing we did in planning *Unique Eats and Eateries of Omaha* was to create a list of restaurants, cafés, and other eatery-related businesses we wanted to include in the book. That initial list exceeded two hundred names. The challenge was to ensure that we included interesting, yet original stories. As with any book of this nature, if your favorite restaurant didn't make it, it wasn't personal or on purpose. We wanted to balance culinary styles and ensure we included a diverse look at the city. Our choices are eateries we enjoy dining at and recommend to people when visiting our city. We did learn about a few new restaurants that are now among our favorites.

In the end, we each have our preferences and favorites. These restaurants are our favorites.

UNIQUE EATS AND EATERIES
OF
OMAHA

AMATO'S CAFÉ AND CATERING

Food seemed to be in Sam Amato's blood. He ran a delicatessen and food stands in Omaha and Minnesota. Moving back to Omaha from Idaho, he ran a catering business from his basement. In turn, Sam decided to open another restaurant in Omaha. He liked a location near Sixtieth and Center because of its proximity to the Aksarben horse racing track and coliseum.

Jockeys, horse walkers, trainers, and fans would dine at the café after it opened its doors in 1993. Aksarben faded and was eventually replaced by a retail and office center as well as a University of Nebraska-Omaha campus expansion, but Amato's Café & Catering stayed. Today, it's run by Sam's widow, Ann, and son Tony, following Sam's passing in 2017.

Popular with an older crowd for a long time, Sam "held court" with regulars, occupying a round table in the middle of the dining room and discussing everything from the day's events to the menu. Later, Amato's saw a huge uptick in younger families and couples coming in for breakfast and lunch, following a 2009 appearance on the Food Network's *Diners, Drive-Ins and Dives*. The restaurant had also appeared on an episode of *Man v. Food*, but it was the Food Network show starring Guy Fieri that launched Amato's popularity with the younger crowd.

Today, longtime diners mix daily with the younger lot, as they're all fans of the unique menu, which offers an Italian spin on breakfast dishes. Included on the menu is an omelet featuring sausage and peppers (known as "The Mistake") as well as ricotta-filled pancakes. Customers have a say in the names of menu items, such as the Mailman Special (created for a local postal carrier), Larry's Volcano

Top left: Ricotta pancakes are a popular breakfast item.

Top right: Amato's cooking is like visiting Grandma.

Bottom left: The unpretentious restaurant was featured on *Diners, Drive-Ins and Dives* in 2009.

Bottom right: Sausage and peppers omelet mixes Italian culinary tradition with American breakfast.

(biscuits and gravy topped with eggs and sausage, named for a guy called Larry), and Rod's 3-2-1 Special (three bacon, two French toast, and one egg).

The restaurant is open 7:00 a.m. to 1:30 p.m. Tuesday through Friday and until 1:00 p.m. on weekends. The Amatos take a day off on Mondays. As Omaha's food scene continues to change, the Amatos look toward the future with their own ideas. Already providing catering, they're considering adding to the food truck scene with their own truck. Who wouldn't like to get a ricotta pancake from a food truck?

6405 Center Street
402-558-5010
amatoscafe.com

MALARA'S ITALIAN RESTAURANT

As a young immigrant to the United States, Caterina Malara faced a young woman's worst nightmare: at the age of thirty-two with four young children, she was widowed. With no true work experience, she knew she had to somehow support her family. She used her talents in the kitchen to make ravioli to sell out of her home.

Born in Italy, her family later moved to Argentina before she immigrated to the United States in 1963. Her husband died in a work-related accident. Her at-home business took off, with people stopping by daily to pick up handmade ravioli. Later, a city inspector told her she couldn't sell out of her home.

Unsure of her future, Caterina soon learned that Rotella's—a longtime Omaha bakery—was moving from its location on Pierce Street and offered her an opportunity to rent a bay. As she built the new Malara's Italian Restaurant, Rotella's eventually planned to sell the building. Offered a loan by a friend, Caterina bought the building. Since opening its doors in 1984, the restaurant at Twenty-first and Pierce streets has provided comfort Italian food, such as spaghetti and meatballs as well as lasagna.

Malara's primarily sold sandwiches when it opened. Since its store was small, they sold out of a window. Originally, they didn't have tables for people to sit at to eat, but her son-in-law later brought her some.

Malara's went on to purchase the next two bays in the building, increasing its dining room size and providing a party room (complete with the ovens from the former bakery). The restaurant is dimly lit, with a beautiful Italian décor, perfect for a date night. The food is delicious. The restaurant continues to make the handmade pasta

Left: Caterina Malara is the matriarch of the restaurant.
Top right: Homemade pasta is a treat at Malara's.
Bottom right: Malara's is located in Rotella's former bakery.

with the same pasta machine Caterina used to make ravioli in her home. The pasta has dumpling-like consistency, while the marinara sauce has a unique sweet taste. Don't ask the staff for the recipe, as Caterina doesn't use measuring cups or spoons when creating dishes.

As Caterina steps back a little in her daily activities in the restaurant, a daughter and granddaughter help run Malara's, ensuring a smooth transition when she's ready to stop and smell the roses.

2123 Pierce Street
402-346-8001
malarasitalianrestaurant.com

ETHNIC SANDWICH SHOP

Lodged between old brick buildings along a stretch of Thirteenth Street stands a former Dairy Queen, looking oddly out of place, its picnic tables and parking lot before a background of homes. Such is life in the Little Bohemia neighborhood, the area Ethnic Sandwich Shop calls home.

Opened in 1977 by Fred Orsi—of the city's famous Orsi Bakery clan—the renovated DQ offers diners a casual atmosphere to enjoy a truly ethnic menu. From an Irish corned beef sandwich to authentic Italian pasta, the take-out restaurant maintains a strong presence along the Thirteenth Street corridor.

Orsi sought to have a sandwich shop that would appeal to the neighborhood, with a mix of ethnic groups, such as Czech, Polish, German, and Italian. Among the popular menu items, Polish sausage, Italian sausage and peppers, and meatball sandwiches score high with customers. His homemade mac and cheese is also a favorite.

Tracy Kyler bought the restaurant in 2004 and continued to offer the classics of various cultures. She eventually sold it in mid-2018.

While she owned the shop, Tracy encouraged customers and employees to name sandwiches, including the "Sparky," named by an electrician, and "The Kapone," created by an employee. Tracy asked if they could spell it with a K, honoring the former owners of the defunct Bohemian Café located a few steps north of the sandwich shop.

After placing your order, watch it being made a few feet away. Afterward, take your order and head on your way. Or grab a spot at one of the picnic tables located around the parking lot, enjoying some shade under a tree in front of the shop, or sit along the side of the building away from the wind on a breezy day.

Top left: The shop's sausage and peppers sandwich is among its most popular.

Top right: Ethnic Sandwich Shop is in a converted Dairy Queen building.

Bottom left: Ethnic Sandwich Shop has a small lobby and kitchen.

Bottom right: Meatball sandwich and pasta salad combine for a delicious lunch.

As the Little Bohemia district grows, including new restaurants, a coffee shop, and retail outlets, the future looks bright for the Ethnic Sandwich Shop. Who knows, maybe there will be new sandwiches named after new residents.

1438 South 13th Street
402-422-1040
ethnicsandwich.com

J. COCO

At fifteen years old, Jennifer Coco's first job in the restaurant industry was far from the glamour and spotlight a chef enjoys. She bussed tables at the Baking Company, clearing tables after customers finished their meals. Later, she helped in the kitchen, cutting vegetables. Not bad for a high school girl.

Planning to become a lawyer, Jennifer attended the University of Nebraska in Lincoln, studying political science. She put herself through college by doing what she knew best—waiting tables. As she neared a decision to pursue law school, Jennifer chose to go into the restaurant industry instead.

She returned to Omaha, eventually working at V. Mertz in the Old Market. The upscale restaurant lost its chef one night, and thus her career as a chef began. She and a coworker taught each other how to cook like chefs, studying magazines and books. Her career took off as the chef at Flat Iron Grill downtown, where she spent fourteen years.

The James Beard Award nominee opened her own place— j. coco—in 2012, and the self-taught chef hasn't looked back. Using her experience as a guide, she's built a strong team that strives to provide diners a wonderful experience beyond just a good steak. Offering a clean, inviting atmosphere, diners enjoy lunch or dinner at the highly acclaimed restaurant in the Dundee neighborhood. The menu offers Omaha staples, such as tasty steaks, pork chops, and chicken, while also offering diners a sample of new dishes, including sea bass and seared tuna.

j. coco strives to use farm-to-table ingredients as often as possible. The restaurant uses an on-site organic garden while also working with local farms.

5203 Leavenworth Street
402-884-2626
jcocoomaha.com

Top left: Creative dishes join Nebraska standards on the menu.

Bottom left: The restaurant is packed daily for lunch and dinner.

Right: The Leavenworth Street restaurant has been popular since opening a few years ago.

MODERN LOVE

A noted author with several cookbooks covering all things vegan, from cooking for the holidays to creating vegan cupcakes, Isa Chandra Moskowitz seemingly has done it all. So why would a girl from Brooklyn choose to open a vegan restaurant in Omaha, Nebraska, in the middle of beef country? For love. Isa moved to Omaha to be with her boyfriend. Then, in 2014, she opened Modern Love at its original location on South Fiftieth Street.

Omahans welcomed the vegan restaurant with open arms, as not all residents are die-hard red meat eaters. During its early run, the house was packed and required reservations. Diners, including nonvegans, enjoy everything from appetizers featuring buffalo wings made of seitan (wheat gluten) to Mac and Shews, an entrée starring roasted red pepper cashew cheese, roasted cauliflower, and cornmeal-crusted tofu. The menu includes gluten-free options.

Four years later Modern Love moved to Midtown Crossing, taking up the spot vacated by Chicago Dawg House, which became a food truck. The Midtown location increased Modern Love's seating capacity.

The chef/owner opened a second Modern Love restaurant in her native Brooklyn and splits time between the two locations.

3157 Farnam Street, Suite 7113
402-614-6481
modernloveomaha.com

Top left: Buffalo cauliflower wings may make you rethink your favorite wings.

Top right: Modern Love has a prime location at Midtown Crossing.

Bottom left: In moving to Midtown Crossing in 2018, Modern Love doubled its seating capacity.

Bottom right: Modern Love is known for its vegan take on poutine, including cashew cheese curds and onion gravy.

LOUIE M'S BURGER LUST

Destiny likely owned Louis Marcuzzo. With a family history in the Omaha restaurant scene dating back to the early 1900s and Louis having worked in some of those places, Louie M's Burger Lust seemed like a logical career choice.

His grandmother ran a restaurant in Little Italy, opening in the mid-1930s. She ran it through the 1950s, when two of Louis's uncles took it over. Louis started helping them when he was ten. His dad opened Johnny's Lunchroom near Tenth and Burlington and ran it for about twenty-two years. It was here that Louis truly cut his chops in the restaurant business.

It wasn't until his mid-forties when Louis left the corporate world to open what would become Louie M's in the Vinton district. In 1980, he opened a catering business, buying the remains of a small diner to use as a prep location. He provided catering services in the area, including day care centers. One day some local shopkeepers noticed him in the diner and stopped by for coffee. Coffee soon turned into donuts and coffee. Later, he brought in a toaster for requests.

Louis decided to open the diner full-time. With a small counter, the diner also featured tables and booths. Offering breakfast and lunch—highlighted by his burgers—Louie M's caught on quickly with locals. About six years later, he bought the building next door and expanded the restaurant.

As he celebrates nearly forty years in business, Louis's two sons help run the restaurant. As he "winds" down his career, he lets them create weekend menus. Louie M's Burger Lust is open for dinner Thursday through Saturday nights, so the younger Marcuzzos design menus with such items as chicken parmesan, breaded Italian sirloin, and a classic Reuben. Of course, the popular burgers are also on the dinner menu.

Top left: South Omaha's sports and cultural history are on display inside the restaurant.

Bottom left: Located along Vinton Street, Louie M's has been a neighborhood favorite since the 1980s.

Top right: A mural welcomes visitors to Louie M's.

Middle right: A jalapeno cheeseburger is a delicious option at Louie M's Burger Lust.

Bottom right: Louie M's started inside this diner.

1718 Vinton Street
402-449-9112
louiemsburgerlust.com

SHIRLEY'S DINER

Don't be surprised to see Doug Fackler take a guitar off the wall, sit down next to you, and play a few riffs. Once a performer, always a performer. Such is life for the face of Shirley's Diner. The former rock-and-roll guitarist/singer grew tired of playing night gigs and sought something different. When his brother-in-law tipped him about Shirley's, the musician became a restaurateur.

Taking over the diner in a strip mall, with neighbors such as a renovated movie theater, now serving as a church, and a dive bar, Doug and his wife, Denise, a former singer of their band, bought Shirley's in 1993. Today, Doug manages the retro-themed restaurant with one of their sons. In 2017, the Facklers moved Shirley's to a former Pizza Hut building a short walk from the original location.

As soon as you walk into Shirley's, you know you've headed down a nostalgia highway. With records lining the walls as well as old miniature jukeboxes hanging on the wall at tables, the restaurant proudly shares its music influence. With posters of Elvis Presley and other stars scattered about, Shirley's reminds people of a diner from the 1950s. All that's missing are roller-skating servers.

Diners enjoy a friendly atmosphere. Even on your first visit, servers treat you like you're old friends. Some of the regulars even get hugs before they leave after enjoying a delicious homestyle meal. The menu offers diners a wide selection of options.

Hand-breaded chicken fried steak serves as Shirley's breakfast staple. They've sold more than a million over the years, Doug likes to joke. The homemade biscuits and gravy are both freshly prepared.

Lunch and dinner menu options include handmade onion rings among other homestyle selections. The cheese Frenchy rates as one of the more popular menu items. With other items, such as chicken fried chicken and pork tenderloin among the entrées, diners also

Top left: Shirley's Diner invites customers for a trip down memory lane with its entrance.

Top right: Breakfast at Shirley's is a must.

Bottom left: Shirley's Diner presents a nostalgic trip with your meal.

Bottom right: Longtime customers are treated like family.

enjoy fried catfish and freshly made burgers, including a three-cheese burger. Shirley's Diner uses Omaha Steaks for their meats.

Trading in his rock-and-roll career for a culinary career may seem like night and day, but for Doug, it's a different style of performance. Now he can grab a cup of coffee and strum a few chords for customers while enjoying time at home with the family.

13838 R Plaza
402-896-6515
shirleysdiner.com

JOHN'S GRECIAN DELIGHT

Emigrating to the United States in 1971, newlyweds John and Demetra Sakkas planned to live here for a few years and then return to their Greek homeland. Ten years later, the couple opened a restaurant at Bellevue's Southroads Mall, a bustling retail and entertainment center a short drive from just about anywhere in the Omaha Metro area.

At one time, John's Grecian Delight stood out among the mall's dining spots, with lines running outside the restaurant and down a hallway, Demetra says.

Times change. Southroads Mall's stores and restaurants eventually closed in the early 2000s, a victim of the area's changing economy, but John's Grecian Delight stayed. Clothing stores, such as JCPenney, and other markets were replaced by computer companies as part of the Southroads Technology Center. The Greek restaurant—home to the best gyro in the Metro—continued to serve its loyal customers. TD Ameritrade, an investment company created by the Ricketts family (current owners of the Chicago Cubs), opened a large office at the former mall. That helped keep the restaurant busy.

Then TD Ameritrade moved to its skyscraper corporate offices in West Omaha. John's Grecian Delight saw its business slip. There were opportunities to move to another area of Bellevue, even Omaha, but John declined those overtures, primarily due to his loyalty to their customers.

As times started to get tough, social media helped rescue the eatery. A Facebook group—Taste of Bellevue—hosted a foodie event at the restaurant. Members' posts rekindled support for John's Grecian Delight. Since that outing, the restaurant has enjoyed—if not overflowing crowds of yesteryear—steady business.

Today, the main customers are teachers from the Christian school located at the technology center, IT workers, military members from Offutt Air Force Base and STRATCOM, and other locals.

Top left: John's Grecian Delight is considered the top gyro restaurant in the area.

Top right: John's attracts a nice lunch crowd during the week.

Bottom: Located in a once-thriving shopping mall, John's Grecian Delight stands out among its current neighbors.

The couple are glad they stayed, considering their regular customers "like one big family," Demetra says. John lives for the restaurant, she says. He's there before the sun comes up and long after it sets.

The menu offers gyros, Greek salads, burgers, and daily specials all at affordable prices. The couple like keeping prices low, Demetra says. "The kids are grown. We're OK," she says.

As Bellevue changes, one constant remains at Southroads—John's Grecian Delight—and John, a former Greek policeman who always dreamed of having his own restaurant, plans to keep it that way.

1001 Fort Crook Road North, Suite 110
402-731-8022
facebook.com/Johns-Grecian-Delight

SURFSIDE CLUB

Fans love the Surfside Club for a variety of reasons—the "world-famous" chicken, the great local music scene, or the annual "mooning" of customers. Whatever the reason, people have flocked to the restaurant and lounged along the Missouri River just a few miles north of the Mormon Bridge on River Road for nearly seventy years.

Opened in 1952, the Surfside hosted Big Band-era bands along with the sounds of wannabe Frank Sinatras, Mel Tormes, and any other famous crooner that may have come along. Eventually, the local music tastes acquired a more rock 'n' roll flavor, and local bands covering songs by the Beatles, Rolling Stones, Bob Seger, and the Eagles eventually took over the stage.

Through it all, appetites craved the "world famous" fried chicken, still finger-lickin' good after all these years. Served with an appetizer of corn fritters (fried dough balls with pieces of corn inside), a meal at the Surfside needs to be on everyone's Omaha culinary bucket list. With a limited menu, diners can also enjoy burgers and pork tenderloin sandwiches.

As diners enjoy a summertime meal outdoors on the patio—surrounded by palm trees (not many places in Omaha feature palm trees)—it's common to be greeted by people "mooning" them as they pass by on speeding boats on the river. The tradition of passers-by dropping their swim bottoms to flash their backsides to diners grew from the owners' decision more than forty years ago to close the marina at the restaurant. Boaters displayed their displeasure to the decision by "mooning" the restaurant. It grew into a tradition as the years passed.

In 2011, a major flood decimated parts of the Midwest along the Missouri River corridor. Omaha wasn't immune. Although flood waters didn't damage Surfside as it did neighboring attractions and

Top left: The Surfside Club is the only place you'll likely find palm trees outside in Omaha.

Top right: Pork tenderloin sandwiches are one of the items on the menu.

Bottom left: Fried chicken is a must at Surfside.

Bottom right: Watching games or enjoying time together makes for a fun outing.

buildings, the restaurant was closed due to the flooding. It remained closed along with much of the area until 2013. It was then that Mike Walker took over as the owner. Mike had owned the former Boondockers bar in northwest Omaha and had wanted to buy Surfside for more than twenty years.

With Mike at the helm, Surfside continues to provide a fun, entertaining atmosphere that attracts people wanting good food, good music, and a good time. Mike loves the charm of Surfside and its history. The restaurant offers a family-friendly experience, with Mother's Day and Father's Day among the busiest days of the season.

Surfside Club's season opens in the spring and runs through late October.

14445 North River Drive
402-457-4000
thesurfsideclub.com

HAROLD'S KOFFEE HOUSE

From a shoe store employee to the patriarch of a cooking family, Harold Halstead found his niche when he started working for a hamburger company after serving in the army during World War II. After working for Harkert's Hamburgers in Omaha, he went into business with two other men, opening the Koffee House restaurant chain in Omaha.

Later, after the Koffee House owners parted company, Harold decided to open his own place in the Florence area. After Harold's Koffee House opened in 1958, it quickly became a local landmark for people looking for an outstanding breakfast or lunch. Keeping the "Koffee" spelling, the restaurant opened a few blocks north of its current location at Thirtieth and State, where Harold's Koffee House attracted people for a decade. Then, in 1968, he moved the restaurant to its current spot. People fondly recall watching Harold cook with a white papered flight-style cap on his head.

When people ask others for directions to Harold's, they're often told to look for the black-lettered FOOD sign with the orange background. While some may think it's an advertising gimmick, chef Matt Bohnenkamp—Harold's grandson—says a salesman told his grandfather it would be an attention-getter. It's been there since the late 1960s.

Harold's tale involves a true family business. From Harold to Matt, three generations of Halsteads have worked at the restaurant. His children worked at the diner as children, from kitchen work to bussing tables. After Harold passed away in 1992, son Tom and daughter Nancy took over. Matt has since taken over Tom's share of the restaurant, but you'll still see Tom sitting in at a table near the kitchen entrance, the same spot Harold occupied, helping out as needed and kibitzing with diners, some of them longtime customers.

Top left: Harold's Koffee House has been part of Florence since opening its doors.

Top right: Harold's old-fashioned dining room is part of its six-decade-old charm.

Bottom left: There's something nostalgic about eating at a counter.

Bottom right: The Susie's Special is a top-seller.

With a menu of homestyle cooking, diners find it difficult to choose the right meal, as each item is delicious. The "Susie's Special" may be the most popular item. Named for one of Harold's daughters, the "special" consists of hand-cut and shredded hash browns, two eggs cooked in, with diced onions. Pauline, their mom, made it for her once when she was ill, and it found its way onto the menu.

8327 North 30th Street
402-451-9776
haroldskoffeehouse.com

"If you get up in the morning and want to go to work, it's better than having to go to work."

21

DAIRY TWIST

What started as a short-term investment turned into a nearly four-decade love affair for Dan Kouba. His uncle and a friend owned the Dairy Twist in Bellevue for about a year before Dan and his father decided to take it over. They signed a one-year lease, with Dan planning to move on after the year was up.

His father was an entrepreneur, having once owned Club Bellevue. The father-son team decided to roll the dice. As a college student without a major, Dan liked the idea of working with his father. Living in Bellevue, which was a much smaller city in 1980, the Koubas thought they could make the ice cream joint work. Along with nearby Offutt Air Force Base, Dairy Twist catered to the local community.

Offering fresh homemade food, such as pork tenderloin and burgers as well as their own spin on ice cream—Dan says Dairy Twist was the first in the Omaha area to crumble up Oreo cookies and put them in ice cream—Dairy Twist provides a truly Bellevue experience. Dan appreciates visits from regulars who dine at Dairy Twist at least once a week. That tells him the staff does a good job preparing meals and ice cream treats as well as treating the customers decently.

2211 Lincoln Road
402-292-1303
facebook.com/Dairy-Twist-104996326210656

Left: Don't forget dessert at Dairy Twist.

Top right: The eatery's ambience is casual.

Middle right: The Dairy Twist has been a Bellevue staple since 1980.

Bottom right: Pork tenderloin and French fries are a popular combination.

eCREAMERY ICE CREAM & GELATO

From its earliest days, eCreamery seemed destined to become a major player in the ice cream world. Opening the store in 2007, Becky App and Abby Jordan sought to create a business where they could express themselves while offering customers a quality product. Having worked together at local jewelry giant Borsheim's, Abby longed to work with food, whereas Becky dreamed of running her own business. Along with an investor, they bought a former ice cream parlor in the Dundee neighborhood.

Trying to create a name for the ice cream parlor at Fiftieth and Underwood Avenue, the duo seemed intent on going with Dundee Creamery. Their investor had another idea. Having purchased a domain name, eCreamery.com, he persuaded the duo to go with that name. In the end, it became the perfect name. eCreamery owns a large stake in online ice cream sales today. Online ice cream, you ask? The company offers a variety of online frozen treats, focusing on special occasions and customized labels as well as personally created flavors.

In the early days, Abby recalls counting the daily cash register take at the boutique ice cream parlor. One cold winter day, they had about $30 in sales. Who would have known then that eCreamery would go on to become a multimillion-dollar operation?

As word of the Omaha online ice cream shop spread, Becky and Abby found their business being featured on The Food Network and in such magazines as *Oprah*, but it may have been an appearance on ABC Television's *Shark Tank* that put eCreamery on the ice cream map. While the duo didn't get a deal with any of the Sharks, business dramatically improved both at the store and online.

Left: eCreamery creates personalized ice cream pints.

Middle: eCreamery makes its ice cream in-house.

Right: eCreamery's boutique shop is its only store.

eCreamery became known for giving whacky names to some oddball flavors. Becky and Abby promoted their appearance on *Shark Tank* by naming flavors after the show, such as Shark Bait, a premium sea salt caramel gelato with chocolate-covered pretzels. They've also named special flavors for each of the eight teams playing in the College World Series each year.

Photos of local billionaire Warren Buffett and music legend Sir Paul McCartney sitting on a bench outside the store enjoying their eCreamery ice cream went viral, boosting store and online sales.

As eCreamery became more successful, the business outgrew its humble office and production space at the parlor. A new investor replaced the original investor in 2016, and the company moved its operations to southwest Omaha. Gone are the days of lugging supplies through a cramped hallway. Now, distributors unload their supplies at a warehouse.

While eCreamery has grown from the days of $30 in the till to becoming a major player in online sales, the company continues to keep its only ice cream parlor in Dundee, where it keeps attracting ice cream aficionados and families looking for an ice cream treat.

5001 Underwood Avenue
402-934-3888
ecreamery.com

RAY'S ORIGINAL BUFFALO WINGS

Buffalo wings fans suffered a loss when local favorite Ray's Original Wings closed up shop around 2000, about ten years after introducing Omaha to the western New York delicacy. Then, fifteen years after closing, Ray's returned and quickly regained its position as Omaha's favorite wing joint.

Working with a mentor from Colorado, Ray and Lori Bullock opened the restaurant in a strip center near Ninety-sixth and Q streets. The mentor shared wing sauce recipes with them as well business tips. Their adventure began when Ray smelled wings while the family was in Colorado Springs attending a sports event for one of their children.

After nearly ten years in business, life got in the way of the original Ray's. Ray received a promotion at his "other" full-time job, and their children grew from toddlers roaming about the restaurant, as Lori and employees dished up the mild to raging-hot spicy sauces. With their children becoming active in sports and school activities, the Bullocks chose family and Ray's sales career over running the restaurant daily. Eventually, the Bullocks decided to close the eatery.

Fast-forward to 2016. Having worked in telecommunications for nearly three decades, Ray's bosses offered him early retirement. He took it. While plotting his next step in life, Ray, now in his mid-fifties, went for a motorcycle ride with a friend. That friend, who happened to own a South Omaha bar, mentioned to him that she wanted to use an empty space in her bar for a kitchen. They each said, almost simultaneously, that Ray's Wings should make a return. So, a short time later, Ray and his son, Tom, made buffalo wings out of the small kitchen at Rhonda Lemmond's Lemon Drop Bar.

Left: Buffalo wings range from mild flavor to flaming hot.
Right: Ray's is the official Buffalo Bills bar in Omaha.

After three years, Ray wanted to expand his business to include a bar as well as a larger kitchen. When an opportunity arose to take over a vacated spot at Midtown Crossing, the Bullocks jumped at it. With minor renovations, Ray's Original Wings opened in a prime location in the retail and entertainment district. With large-screen televisions dotting the walls, sports fans enjoy grabbing a basket of wings and enjoying a few drinks as they watch their favorite teams on TV. Ray's serves as the official bar for Buffalo Bills fans.

Lots of Bills fans call Omaha home. When the now defunct Western Electric Company relocated employees from western New York, hundreds transferred to the Omaha plant in the 1970s. Their children and now grandchildren became Bills fans. Ray estimates that on any given NFL Sunday about one hundred of the one hundred and fifty seats are occupied by Bills fans. And that's OK with the lifelong Bills fan, whose own family hailed from Buffalo. His mother moved the family there from California during his childhood following his father's passing.

Ray arrived in Omaha in the late 1970s through an Air Force assignment. He never left, and Omaha's culinary scene is better off for it.

120 South 31st Avenue, Suite 5103
402-884-5300
rayswings.com

ORSI'S ITALIAN BAKERY AND PIZZERIA

As an eight-year-old, Jim Hall wrapped bread and helped with Orsi's Sunday deliveries. In return, he would scamper home with his paycheck—a couple of loaves of bread. Such was life in Omaha's Little Italy, where almost everyone has an Orsi's-related story. For Jim, however, he would grow up to become the first nonfamily member to own Orsi's Bakery and Pizzeria. Though not related by blood, Jim and others like him could have been considered part of the brood, hanging out and working there as children.

A mainstay in the neighborhood since Alfonso Orsi opened the doors in 1919, Orsi's pizza attracts fans from across Omaha. The handmade Sicilian pizza, which is cut into squares, ranks among the best in the city, with people calling in orders early on weekends. They'll even stand in line and wait to get their order in. Its menu also offers goudarooni, which is a double-crusted pizza. With limited seating, it's best to order takeout.

Orsi's first opened near Twenty-first and Poppleton, but Alfonso moved the bakery to its current location in 1934. A 1997 fire destroyed the bakery, but the neighborhood's response in helping to quickly rebuild it solidified Orsi's role as the center of Little Italy.

Jim and Bob Orsi Jr. bought the business from Bob's father in 2006. Then, in 2010, Jim became the first non-Orsi to own the bakery.

Orsi's also serves as a pseudo South Omaha Hall of Fame, with pictures of Italian-American athletes, politicians, and celebrities.

621 Pacific Street
402-345-3438
orsibakery.com

Left: A 1997 fire destroyed Orsi's, but the neighborhood worked together to rebuild it.

Top right: Omahans consider Orsi's one of the best pizzas in the city.

Bottom right: Orsi's is the place to go to get some of the best imported Italian food in Omaha.

GERDA'S GERMAN RESTAURANT AND BAKERY

As a child growing up in Augsburg, Germany, Gerda Bailey lived through the reign of Adolf Hitler. Her daughter, Kim Reefe, recalls stories of Gerda and her aunt running during air raids, as bombs dropped from the sky during World War II. It seemed a lifetime from that Bavarian city to Omaha, Nebraska.

Gerda passed away in mid-2018 at the age of eighty-three. With the love people had for her and the popularity of her German menu, Kim decided to keep the restaurant open, starting a new generation for Gerda's.

The matriarch lived a full life. When she grew up, Gerda married an American serviceman, and they had two sons together. Following their time in Germany, the family was assigned to a base in North Carolina. After their divorce, Gerda married another serviceman, this time an airman in the Air Force.

During their marriage, Gerda learned that her husband had a daughter—Kim—who was living with her mother. Gerda answered the phone one night and was told she needed to come and take Kim, a baby, from an unsafe environment. She didn't hesitate and drove to the house and brought Kim home to live with the couple.

The family arrived in Omaha in 1972, when her husband was assigned to Offutt Air Force Base. Gerda adopted Kim when she was two years old and started working at Rotella's Bakery.

Gerda decided to open her own bakery in 1976 at its Leavenworth location. While working on opening Gerda's bakery, the couple divorced. Kim, seven, stayed with her mother, spending time with a family friend while Gerda worked in the bakery and handled the family's issues.

Top left: A mural provides a backdrop in the dining room.

Top middle: The bakery was the first section of Gerda's when it opened.

Top right: Gerda celebrating. Photo provided by Kim Reefe.

Bottom left: Bratwurst with spaetzle and sauerkraut.

Bottom right: Welcome to Gerda's.

Gerda's bakery caught on quickly, as she started supplying local supermarkets and cafés with fresh pastries and German treats. Later, as grocery stores started to bring their baking operations in-house, Gerda looked to new revenue sources. She then added the restaurant portion to Gerda's Authentic German Restaurant and Bakery.

The restaurant remains the lone German-centric eatery in the Omaha area, offering such dishes as bratwurst and schnitzel served with sides of spaetzle, red cabbage, German potato salad, and dumplings. The bakery also serves freshly prepared morning treats, including kolaches.

As a new era begins with Gerda's, Kim seeks to keep history alive, as the restaurant continues to host its annual Oktoberfest reminiscent of the world-famous Munich celebration. Featuring music, German bier, and lots of food, thousands of people attend the event in mid-September.

5180 Leavenworth Street
402-553-6774
gerdasgermanrestaurant.com

METRO COMMUNITY COLLEGE SAGE STUDENT BISTRO

Many talented chefs and high-level cooks enjoy outstanding reputations around Omaha restaurants. Several of them learned under the tutelage of professors and teachers, who were fine chefs and cooks themselves, as part of the culinary arts program at Metropolitan Community College. Included among those who have cut their teeth in the program are Paul and Jessica Urban, owners of popular Block 16, who met while attending MCC.

As part of the curriculum, students work as servers, chefs, and managers at the school's Sage Student Bistro. Located on the school's historic Fort Omaha campus, students run a fully functioning restaurant that rivals any around town, with a beautiful décor and quality service. From the time student staffers greet diners at the entrance and escort them to their table, they ensure that each person feels as though they are the center of their undying attention. Servers don white shirts and black slacks, with a black apron professionally worn.

With impeccable service, the menu offers an outstanding selection of sandwiches and entrées, along with daily specials. The lunch and dinner menus differ, as dinner is presented in a variety of courses. Dinner is served on elegantly white tableclothed tables and requires a reservation. It also includes a limited wine list.

5730 North 30th Street
531-622-2328
mccneb.edu/sagestudentbistro

Top: Sandwiches and other entrees are among the dishes created by student chefs.

Bottom: Student-run Sage Bistro competes with local restaurants with an amazing menu.

FAT SHACK BBQ

You'd think that with more than twenty years of experience cooking barbecue, there's not much else Cary Dunn needs to know about preparing the perfect rib or brisket. To the Kansas native, however, he and the BBQ world continue to evolve. If Cary needs to evolve much more, diners at Fat Shack BBQ are in for even more treats.

With a lunchtime line that runs out the door and down the sidewalk in front of other stores in a North Omaha shopping center, it solidifies Fat Shack BBQ's reputation as the best barbecue restaurant in Omaha. The restaurant also offers a lunch hour special featuring a cafeteria-style menu, where customers can order cuts of meat and sides. With its BBQ Neapolitan-style pizza popular, Cary ensures it's ready at lunchtime so customers don't have to cut short lunch hours while they wait to order. The restaurant's top seller isn't even BBQ. The Shack Attack is a basket of French fries loaded with nacho cheese, jalapenos, BBQ sauce, shredded cheese, sour cream, and one meat choice.

Fat Shack BBQ struck gold when it opened near Thirtieth and Webber streets in 2013. Starting as a food truck that set up weekends in the parking lot of a former Goodwill store, Fat Shack gained an immediate following. Deep lines of people stood in all types of weather for Cary's Texas-style BBQ. Using the right type of wood to smoke turkey, chicken, ribs, and brisket, Cary starts early in the day, so food is ready around 11:00 a.m.

After operating the food truck for a few years, the Dunns had an opportunity in 2016 to expand and open a full-service restaurant. Having operated three restaurants in the Wichita area before moving to Omaha in 2012, they knew what to expect in moving to a brick-and-mortar business. They found the perfect spot, basically across the street at the Webber Place shopping center. Taking over a former

Top left: Fat Shack has an eclectic art display.

Top right: Cary Dunn slices brisket.

Bottom left: Burnt ends are a popular menu item.

Bottom right: Fat Shack BBQ expanded over the past few years to increase seating.

restaurant location, the Dunns later added a second bay, creating a larger dining room and the cafeteria area.

From using the right wood for cooking to the best rub for the perfect taste, the world of barbecue challenges the cook to stay ahead of the game and continue to create delicious barbecue that keeps bringing people back.

7440 North 30th Street
402-639-7275
fatbbqshack.biz

JONES BROS. CUPCAKES

From a conversation around the family's kitchen table arose one of Omaha's most popular cupcake shops. Bill and Brad Jones, along with family members, launched their concept for Jones Bros. Cupcakes as a "dessert restaurant." They opened their first location in Aksarben Village in 2010 near the former horse racing track and concert venue.

Steps away from a monument dedicated to Triple Crown winner Omaha, Jones Bros. also won, quickly establishing itself as one of THE places to go for great desserts, including cupcakes and cakes, even cheesecake. Made from scratch, cupcakes include fan favorites red velvet, vanilla, and strawberries and cream. Their cupcakes consistently win local accolades, having been named as the best in Omaha six times. Featured on national television programs, including Food Network's *Cupcake Wars*, a judge described Bill's Valentine's Day display as an "edible valentine."

With competition from local restaurants, Jones Bros. Cupcakes added sandwiches, soups, and salads to its menu. With some of the freshest and best-tasting food in the retail and entertainment district, expect a line at the door for orders. Ordering flows quickly, however, and diners enjoy their food or dessert within minutes of sitting down. You can also order specialized coffees, beer, and wine with your meal.

While the original location continues to anchor the franchise, Jones Bros. Cupcakes has also expanded to two more locations in Omaha—Lakeside and Westroads' Flagship Commons.

2121 South 67th Street
402-884-2253
jonesbroscupcakes.com

Left: Jones Bros. Cupcakes has won television baking competitions.

Top right: Jones Bros. was one of the first eateries in Aksarben Village.

Middle right: Sandwich and soup combinations are available.

Bottom right: Enjoy a salad at Jones Bros. before grabbing a cupcake.

ALPINE INN

People visit the Alpine Inn for the fried chicken. They stay to watch the raccoons devour the leftovers. "Dining with the raccoons" remains popular with tourists as well as locals.

Feeding the raccoons started with Carl and Viola Roberts, former owners of the inn. The original owners of Alpine Inn installed a small wood-burning stove to cook hamburgers, and Carl and Viola expanded to a full kitchen, which is still used today, to add chicken and shrimp to the menu.

With the bar enjoying good business, Carl wondered about ways to handle the growing amount of garbage, so he decided to start dumping the leftovers for area raccoons to eat. He took a couple of old wooden boxes and attached them to a tree, creating a dining platform. Raccoons and feral cats started showing up daily to enjoy the fine dining. The rest, as they say, is history. What started as a way to get rid of leftover food turned into a tourist attraction.

In 1973, Glen Robey bought the Alpine Inn when Carl and Viola suggested he take over. An auto mechanic at the time, Glen owned two gas stations of his own. He kept them for another two years until he decided his investment would work out. Meanwhile, he kept up the tradition of throwing out leftovers for the animals.

Today, raccoons and cats travel up to two miles a day to enjoy chicken remains, French fries, and burgers. Animals start arriving near sunset. As they gather—up to seventy or more raccoons on some nights—human diners also meet at the Alpine Inn to enjoy some of the best fried chicken in the United States according to some websites. Glen also recommends the burgers.

It's best to arrive early if you only want to dine there. If you're interested in watching the raccoons—and hundreds of people are nightly—it's recommended to visit closer to sunset, but prepare for a wait to get a table. In the meantime, join others standing next to

Left: Glen Robey has owned Alpine Inn since 1973.

Middle: A raccoon enjoys a meal before others arrive.

Right: Fried chicken is the restaurant's top seller.

the floor-to-ceiling windows and watch as the trash bandits and wild cats show up without reservations for the nightly feeding.

Glen has enjoyed owning the Alpine Inn for more than four decades. He's watched his children and now grandchildren help out and learn the business, from bussing tables to serving customers to running the bar. His role has changed too.

"I'm like the greeter at Walmart," Glen says. " I sit up front and talk to the people and tell them thanks for coming."

Alpine Inn has different hours based on the season, including being closed on Mondays during the winter, so it's a good idea to check the bar's Facebook page before planning your visit. The Alpine Inn also doesn't accept credit/debit cards—only cash, but it does have an ATM on-site.

10405 Calhoun Road
402-451-9988
facebook.com/Alpine-Inn-Home-of-the Wildlife-140251589348630

One More Round

Glen is a member of the Nebraska Auto Racing Hall of Fame following a successful career as a race car driver around regional tracks.

FOOD TRUCKS

There's something about reaching up and taking a sandwich through the window of the truck and then finding a spot on the grass or sidewalk to sit and enjoy your meal. Today, food trucks present a great alternative to restaurants as a place to grab a quick meal. Omaha's food truck scene has exploded over the past decade, with nearly three dozen trucks, trailers, and food carts scattered around the city.

What once resembled playing a game of cat and mouse when trying to find out where the trucks set up daily, improved use of social media platforms has almost eliminated that issue. The food truck industry also united to work together in supporting each other. Following issues with some brick-and-mortar restaurants and the city government, food trucks are better embraced downtown, including a weekly gathering on Thursdays. It's common to find more than a dozen food trucks set up near the public library at Fifteenth and Farnam streets.

In addition, several neighborhoods, including Dundee, Benson, and Blackstone, host food truck rodeos, setting up picnic tables, and even providing entertainment as part of the event. Hundreds of people attend the rodeos, creating an almost festival-like atmosphere.

Omaha's food truck landscape covers a gambit of palates, from Cajun to barbecue to fish and chips. A Taste of New Orleans considers itself Omaha's most authentic Cajun eatery on wheels. Chef Lee and his family left New Orleans during Hurricane Katrina in 2005. Relocating to Omaha to stay with family, Chef decided the Big O was the perfect spot for him to open a food truck offering the family's favorite food. A Taste of New Orleans earned a solid following that continues today. You can regularly find the food truck in the Canfield Plaza parking lot. Chef Lee also participates in the

Left: Food trucks' popularity has skyrocketed in Omaha over the past few years.

Right: There's something fun about taking your food from a truck's window.

downtown Food Truck Thursday as well as some of the rodeos. From its Po Boy to jambalaya, diners enjoy a true taste of New Orleans.

With some of Omaha's food trucks developing a loyal following, they may consider opening a brick-and-mortar eatery. Taqueria el Rey did so in 2004 after operating a food truck for a few months. Today, the Mexican restaurant remains a staple in South Omaha while also operating several food trucks across the city.

While some food truck owners dream of having their own brick-and-mortar restaurants, others use their trucks to continue the legacy of restaurants. Anthony Piccolo's Mobile Venue offers some of the food, such as the prime rib sandwich, that was a customer favorite at the former Piccolo's Italian steakhouse in South Omaha. Once one of Omaha's oldest restaurants, it closed in 2016 after eighty-one years.

As Omaha's food truck scene continues to grow, chefs and cooks have united and worked together to ensure that the industry is represented within the city. They have created the Omaha Food Truck Association, with a Facebook page and website to promote their organization. The OFTA also created an app to help people locate their favorite food truck around the city.

While Omaha's food truck roster grows almost weekly, here's a look at some of the best the city has to offer:

A Taste of New Orleans
facebook.com/atasteofneworleans4u

402BBQ
the402bbq.com

The Dire Lion Grille & Chippy
direlion.com

Anthony Piccolo's Mobile Venue
anthonypiccolos.com

LeBlanc's BBQ, Cajun & More
leblancsbbqandcajun.com

Mosaic Pickle
mosaicpickle.com

Fauxmaha Hot Dogs
facebook.com/fauxmahahotdogs

La Casa Pizzaria Food Truck
lacasapizzaria.net/food-truck

Maria Bonita
mariabonitaonline.com

Smokin Barrel BBQ
facebook.com/smokinbarrelbbq

Taqueria el Rey Food Truck
taqueriaelreydeomaha.com

Tap Dancers Specialty Coffee
tapdancerscoffee.com

Chicago Dawg House
facebook.com/Chicago-Dawg-House-Omaha-118134194926841

Top left: A Taste of New Orleans treats customers to impressive Cajun.

Top right: That's a lot of food.

Bottom left: Piccolo's prime rib sandwich with au jus.

Bottom right: 402 BBQ offers tasty meals.

GREEK ISLANDS

Making their way to America in 1966, brothers Laki "Bill" and George Sgourakis sought a good life in Omaha. Staying with relatives, the duo worked in South Omaha's meat packing plants for nearly two decades, saving money to achieve their dream of opening a restaurant.

The brothers realized their goal when they opened Greek Islands in 1983. Offering a Greek-American menu, diners can enjoy a gyro as well as a hamburger. Opening the original restaurant near Thirty-third and Center, the Sgourakises eventually relocated to the current spot a few blocks east. While Greek Islands offers a relaxed, casual atmosphere, it's common to find people in business suits discussing work sitting next to a couple on a date or a family enjoying a night out.

The brothers seek to provide "Greek comfort" food, featuring homestyle meals. While the gyro is the most popular item, the restaurant's menu includes lamb and Omaha Steaks. Featuring homemade dressings, a meal at Greek Islands takes your taste buds on a journey to the Mediterranean.

3821 Center Street
402-346-1528
greekislandsomaha.com

Top left: The artwork is beautiful at Greek Islands.

Top right: Gyro plate at Greek Islands.

Bottom left: The lamb dinner makes you yearn for a trip to the Greek Isles.

Bottom right: Greek Islands' motif celebrates its Greek heritage.

Looking for a little entertainment with your meal? Try the Flaming Saganaki—OPA!

BROTHER SEBASTIAN'S
STEAK HOUSE AND WINERY

As you exit your vehicle in the parking lot, you're greeted by Gregorian monk chants emanating from speakers outside the building. Viewing the Spanish mission–themed exterior, you then realize you're not in for a typical steakhouse dining experience. Inspired by California's monasteries, Loren Koch opened Brother Sebastian's in 1977.

Appreciative of monks' traditions of kindness and hospitality, Koch seeks the same style of service with Brother Sebastian's. Customers experience that philosophy firsthand as servers, adorned in outfits reminiscent of a monk's robe, provide excellent service throughout the dining experience. Some servers have decades of experience with the restaurant, which is evident in customer service and knowledge of the menu.

Known for some of Omaha's best steaks and prime rib, the restaurant prides itself on offering well-aged cuts of sirloin and ribeye steaks as well as entrées featuring chicken, fresh seafood and fish, and even frog legs. A trip to Brother Sebastian's Steak House & Winery also includes a nostalgic trip through its salad bar. With near ice-cold lettuce, fresh vegetables, and tasty dressings, the salad bar resembles an old-fashioned one.

Diners enjoy their meal in small, dimly lit rooms resembling ones commonly found in a monastery, including a study with books and a wine cellar with barrel lids on the wall. Loren had an intricate role in designing the interior, working alongside the architect, ensuring it met the vision of his Omaha abbey. He intended for people to enjoy a relaxed and comfortable dining experience.

As Omahans woke one February morning in 1996, they learned that a fire had destroyed their favorite steakhouse. Loren

Top left: Each dining room has an abbey theme.

Top right: The restaurant displays monk figurines.

Bottom left: Brother Sebastian's exterior resembles a Spanish mission.

Bottom right: Steak is a popular menu item at Brother Sebastian's.

immediately decided to rebuild. With his designs for the original building still intact, he used them to rebuild, reopening about eight months later. Employees, whom he helped find jobs while the restaurant was closed, returned to the fold. They still joke about who are "pre-fire" and "post-fire" employees.

As he reopened, Loren changed a few things in the restaurant, mainly relocating the wine room to the front of the restaurant, where customers can see the fine wines up close. Loren believes the wines add to Brother Sebastian's ambience.

1350 South 119th Street
402-330-0300
brothersebastians.com

WILSON & WASHBURN

It's not every day that a restaurant uses a madam and one of her top girls as inspiration for its business, but when you're looking to stand out among Omaha's culinary scene, you find a niche. For Jeff and Faith Luby, it was the tale of Omaha's infamous Anna Wilson and her top working girl, Josie Washburn.

Wilson operated a brothel in Omaha's Sporting District, home to the Western town's vice—gambling, prostitution, and organized crime. It actually stood a few blocks east of the restaurant's 1800s-era brick home. She became one of the wealthiest women in town, as she listened to clients discuss property and business plans and then invested in the property ahead of them. The madam supported her team, offering guidance for their futures. Washburn became an author, writing *The Underworld Sewer: A Prostitute Reflects on Life in the Trade, 1871-1909*. A first edition copy of the book hangs on a wall near the entrance.

Open since 2013, the restaurant, which Jeff says is more like a bar with a restaurant, has packed them in. People often dine here before attending a show at the Orpheum Theater or stopping by for a drink afterward. While customers enjoy a laugh over the restaurant's name, it's the menu that keeps bringing them back. Known for its beet chips—yes, beet chips in the style of potato chips—they add to a meal as an appetizer or a side to one of Wilson & Washburn's sandwiches.

Jeff, an Omaha native, left for the Big Apple after attending the University of Nebraska in Lincoln. After fifteen years in New York City, the Lubys wanted to raise their children in the Midwest and returned to the Big O. Faith worked in the mortgage industry, and Jeff decided he wanted to open a bar. The couple are the proud parents of two children.

Top left: Beet chips make for a good appetizer or dinner side.

Top right: The restaurant promotes its namesakes' roles in Omaha's early days.

Bottom left: Wilson & Washburn prides itself on being a neighborhood bar.

Bottom right: Pulled pork egg rolls offer a different take on traditional egg rolls.

But he didn't want just any bar, as the Old Market has plenty of those. Jeff wanted a bar where people could come and relax while enjoying a drink or two. A "Cheers" type of bar, where everyone could know your name (or not). While creating the bar, which features nearly two dozen craft and international brews on tap (no domestic national brands need apply), they also wanted to ensure the restaurant offered great food. The chef hit a "home run" with the menu, Jeff says.

1407 Harney Street

402-991-6950

wilsonandwashburn.com

FARMERS MARKET

In the old days, farmers sold their extra crops at roadside stops, where people might buy sweet corn, tomatoes, potatoes, or fruit. Today, Omahans gather at weekly farmers markets around the Metro area to buy the same homegrown crops, but they may also go home with homemade jams and jellies, bread, handmade jewelry, or locally produced wine.

In the late 1800s and early 1900s, the Old Market served as Omaha's main shopping area for retailers and distributors. Vendors hawked their wares, selling produce in baskets or hanging fresh meat on hooks under the overhangs in front of shops with cast-iron door and window frames. The area's outdoor markets faded over the years, disappearing from the Omaha landscape in the early 1960s.

In 1994, organizers resurrected the Old Market's farmers market. Today, encompassing several streets in the Old Market, the Farmers Market features hundreds of vendors every Saturday morning from early May through mid-October, selling everything from the traditional fruits and vegetables to jams made with bee's honey or even jewelry created from Nebraska-raised corn. It's become a tradition for people to bring their families, including pets, to taste samples and go home with some of the freshest, best-tasting produce you'll find anywhere.

Not to be outdone, other sections of Omaha also have weekly markets. The Old Market Farmers Market organizers also host the Aksarben Village market on Sundays during the season. They also sponsor a Night Market at Midtown Crossing as well as the Aksarben Village Holiday Market. Village Pointe shopping center also has its own on weekends. Area cities have their version of farmers markets, too, including Bellevue, Council Bluffs, and Papillion.

Top left: Hand-picked apples are among locally grown fruit at the Farmers Market.

Top right: Jewelry created from Nebraska-raised corn.

Bottom left: Jams and other products made from honey.

Bottom right: Hundreds of people visit the market weekly during its season.

While the area is home to a dozen or so farmers markets of all sizes, here is a list of a few of the larger ones:

Old Market Farmers Market
519 S 11th Street
402-345-5401
omahafarmersmarket.com

Aksarben Village Farmers Market
67th and Center Streets
402-345-5401
omahafarmersmarket.com

Village Pointe Farmers Market
168th and West Dodge Road
402-505-9773
voterealfood.com

JACK AND MARY'S RESTAURANT

While the restaurant Jack and Mary's has been around since 1975, the original Jack and Mary owned it for only five years. Once known as Cliff's Green Gables, the restaurant's history includes three locations, all within half a mile of each other.

Cliff's called the current Huber Chevrolet dealership home in its early days. The restaurant opened in the 1930s and is the source for the restaurant's still used recipes for fried chicken and gravy. The owners relocated to the Old Mill area in the 1970s after it was sold and renamed for the new owners, Jack and Mary. Ken and Barb Oetter then bought the restaurant in 1980, and their son Kip serves as its manager. Under Kip's guidance, the restaurant provides a comfortable experience, serving homestyle food.

Moving to a shopping strip mall in 1995, Jack and Mary's continues to attract diners, some of whom are longtime fans and have dined there several times a week over the past four decades. Whether it's a working lunch, group outing, or even a wedding party, Jack and Mary's has developed a cultlike following. Kip's goal for attracting a fan base is easy: simplicity and consistency with the menu and service.

655 North 114th Street
402-496-2090
jackandmarysrestaurant.com

Top: Jack and Mary's has served homestyle meals since opening in 1975.

Bottom left: Jack and Mary's dining room is spacious.

Bottom right: Chicken-fried chicken and homemade mashed potatoes are a staple at Jack and Mary's.

JOE TESS PLACE

Pulling carp fresh out of the Missouri River, Joe Tess created the makings of a local favorite, cutting the fish up and selling carp sandwiches for fifteen cents at his local tavern. Who knew that the small fish sandwich shop that started in the 1930s would grow into Omaha's fish giant?

Young Bill Fait worked for Joe Tess helping cut fish. As a grown-up, he opened his own business, Fresh Water Fish. He then bought Joe Tess' in 1965 after the founder passed away. He renamed it Joe Tess Place to honor his mentor and changed the name of his fish business to Fait Fisheries. Operating both businesses at the restaurant, Fait moved away from Missouri River carp to fish found primarily in Minnesota's lakes. His sons now run the business and continue to buy fish from Northern states.

Fried carp dinners remained popular at Joe Tess Place. One of the attractions for the restaurant was a huge aquarium; people often joked about picking their fish.

When the state needed to expand the Kennedy Freeway through South Omaha, it bought Tess'. Fait purchased property a short distance north of the restaurant to build a new Tess'. Instead of adding the aquarium when it opened the new spot in 1985, Fait went with a water fountain.

Joe Tess Place became nationally known over the years, including a 2009 segment on the Food Network's *Diners, Drive-Ins and Dives*, starring Guy Fieri.

Fait passed away in 2013. His son Bill runs the restaurant while the other Faits manage the fishery south of Bellevue. The sons haven't changed much of the business. The fresh fish delivered a few times a week are kept at the fishery until they are marked and delivered to the restaurant for serving. It's possible for someone to

Left: A neon sign attracts diners.

Top right: Joe Tess Place's boat bar is a highlight of the restaurant.

Bottom right: Fish and chips are a great menu choice.

order a carp dinner and have the fish delivered to the restaurant a few minutes later.

The fish industry has struggled over the past few years, Bill says. Catching fish like carp is a challenge and requires more fishing expeditions, but Joe Tess Place's goal is to continue providing carp and other fish, such as rainbow trout and tilapia, for its customers who look forward to a fish dinner, with such sides as fries and coleslaw.

5424 South 24th Street
402-733-4638
joetessplace.com

PETROW'S

Nick and John Petrow emigrated to the United States from Greece in 1898. Eventually settling in Fremont, the brothers opened a candy store downtown in 1903. It would be the first of several investments Nick would make. Two years later Nick and a partner opened a new candy store in the old Brandeis Building in Omaha. A third store—Candyland—opened in Omaha in 1917.

A fire destroyed the Fremont candy shop, so the brothers opened Petrow's Café, a Fremont mainstay for about thirty years.

In 1930, Nick ventured into his own business, selling his two candy stores and opening the Sunset Tea Room in what was West Omaha at the time. The restaurant near Fiftieth and Dodge fell victim to the Great Depression. Petrow ran a few businesses afterward, including the Igloo, an ice cream parlor near Forty-second and Leavenworth, until he took another chance at an eatery. In 1950, he opened what would become the longtime family business. Inside an old gas station, Petrow's was born. It started as a drive-in, complete with carhops. It also included something new to the area—a drive-thru window.

Seven years later Nick's son Chris built a diner next to the drive-in. A parking lot later replaced the drive-in spot. Today, Petrow's consists of four buildings, including the original diner. Chris's son Nick and his wife took over the business in 1992 and continue to run it today.

Petrow's has been a favorite among diners through the years. Known for its homestyle cooking, including fresh burgers, hot beef sandwiches, and pork tenderloins, Petrow's most popular menu item may be its hand-scooped ice cream treats. You can enjoy a sundae featuring a variety of toppings, such as strawberry and chocolate.

Top left: Petrow's sign along Center Street.

Top right: The roast beef sandwich with mashed potatoes at Petrow's.

Bottom: Petrow's dining room is full during any meal.

Petrow's "Clown" sundae is a throwback to its Fremont candy store heritage. Consisting of vanilla and chocolate layered ice cream, it's topped with chocolate and marshmallow syrup, and sprinkled with Spanish nuts.

5914 Center Street
402-551-0552
petrows.com

WHISK + MEASURE

Having a career as a numbers person, Beth Brown used baking as an outlet. After deciding to give up working full-time as an actuary and return to Omaha, she decided to open her own bakery in 2016.

Whisk + Measure isn't your typical bakery. Home to all types of baking, Beth and her team pride themselves on creating cakes and treats that include vegan, paleo, and keto diets. They also offer gluten-free and dairy-free options.

Whisk + Measure seeks to ensure that customers enjoy their cakes whether they're vegan or traditional style. The neat thing about having a bakery like Whisk + Measure in Omaha is that it serves a base that has been underserved in the past.

While cakes, cupcakes, and cheesecakes are among the most popular items the bakery creates for its customers, visiting the bakery is a trip down baking memory lane. With muffins, scones, cookies, and bear claws among the items available at the counter, grab a cup of coffee from its roasting partner Reboot and enjoy a treat while visiting with friends in its spacious seating area.

2505 South 133rd Plaza
402-502-0004
whiskandmeasure.com

Top left: Whisk + Measure's baked goods and coffee make for a nice break.

Top right: Vegan and gluten-free treats are available, including cupcakes.

Bottom left: Whisk + Measure provides a nice setting for meeting friends.

Bottom right: Cookies are great options at Whisk + Measure.

Interested in how to decorate beautiful cakes and cookies yourself? Sign up for one of the many classes at Whisk + Measure.

CONEFLOWER CREAMERY

Coneflower Creamery's "Farm to Cone" mantra tastes as good as it sounds. Located in the Blackstone District, the eatery offers ice cream created from locally sourced ingredients, including milk and cream. Fruit raised in the area is used for special flavors.

The shop opened a couple of years ago inside a small space on Farnam Street in a newly developed area. It's basically a take-out ice cream shop, with limited seating inside. The main goal is to serve up to twenty unique flavors, such as handmade strawberry, dark chocolate, and vanilla bean. Customers can also buy cookies and ice cream sandwiches with their cones or dishes. Working with local farmers, chefs Brian Langbehn and Katie Arant ensure they use the best ingredients in their creations.

The duo met while working at the downtown 801 Chophouse. Chef Brian learned ice cream making while working at a Chicago restaurant. As the executive chef at 801 Chophouse, he hired Katie as the pastry chef. As the two shared their dreams for the future, it seemed inevitable that they should open an ice cream shop together.

Using the Coneflower as a symbol, the eatery celebrates its Midwest heritage. With purple petals, the wildflower is commonly found on the prairie.

3921 Farnam Street
402-913-2399
coneflowercreamery.com

Top left: Coneflower's ice cream is made in-house.

Top right: Chef Brian Langbehn scoops a cone while artisan Katie Arant watches her creation being served.

Bottom left: Though it's in a small building, Coneflower is packed with visitors.

Bottom right: Ice cream comes in cones or bowls.

BRONCO'S

Omaha's first fast-food restaurant refuses to change. Since opening its doors in 1959, Bronco's seeks to provide a quality meal at a good price.

The family-owned business, founded by Bill Barnes and now owned and managed by son Steve and grandson Blake, opened its drive-in near Fort Omaha. During its heyday, it's believed Bronco's had about twenty locations around the country, including five in the Omaha area. Though the original location closed several years ago, Bronco's remains popular with locals. It still has two locations in Omaha—one in Midtown and one in West Omaha. People enjoy the nostalgia that dining at the restaurant brings as well as its ambience with pinball games and Western-themed decorations.

As restaurants change menus to remain relevant, Bronco's relies on its decades-old menu to attract customers. Long known for its double cheeseburger, featuring grilled onions and pickles, Bronco's offers customers a simple, yet consistent menu. Its Big Bronco includes two burger patties on a three-piece bun with Bronco's special sauce. The restaurant also hand-cuts and breads its pork tenderloins.

1123 South 120th Street
402-551-7477
broncoburgers.com

Left: Cowboys help provide a western theme.

Top right: Bronco's makes the ordering process simple and quick.

Bottom right: Bronco Burger and fries combination.

LIL BURRO

Shane Ashelford's Lil Burro could easily have been Little Italy, as the former Air Force cook cut his teeth cooking while stationed in Italy. It wasn't until his post-military life that he developed a talent cooking Mexican fare. If he hadn't taken a kitchen job at a Boulder, Colorado, Mexican restaurant, it would have been Omaha's loss.

After settling in Omaha, the Lil Burro owner bought a former convenience store and transformed it into one of the Metro area's best Mexican restaurants. He and his family spend time in their garden behind the restaurant, harvesting about a thousand plants, featuring eleven varieties of peppers, which are used in their cooking. Shane proudly believes that Lil Burro's menu offers some of the freshest and most flavorful dishes in the area.

Lil Burro challenges your taste buds to enjoy a Mexican extravaganza, from the quesadillas with a blend of cheeses to the chili rellenos featuring an Anaheim pepper.

Shane wants diners to have a place where they can be comfortable, relaxing with a nice meal among friends, similar to the television series *Cheers*, which happens to be his favorite show. The Sarpy County restaurant, which is located near Offutt Air Force Base, attracts visitors from the base as well as the community.

12510 South 29th Avenue
402-292-0102
lilburro.net

Top left: Lil Burro creates authentic-tasting Mexican dishes.

Top right: Combining a Mexican flare with traditional American pop art creates a unique ambience.

Bottom left: Located near Offutt Air Force Base, Lil Burro attracts a mix of military and local diners.

Bottom right: Shane Ashelford developed his cooking skills in the Air Force.

PEPPERJAX

Born in Omaha in the early 2000s, Pepperjax provides Philly cheesesteaks that could rival any from Philadelphia. Opened in a strip mall, the original Pepperjax quickly became popular with locals. Before opening for business, founder Gary Rohwer spent a few years trying to create the perfect meat for his cheesesteaks. Once he was happy, the first location opened.

The restaurant eventually expanded to eight locations around the Omaha metro, including its first drive-thru location in Bellevue. As Pepperjax grew in popularity, the chain expanded to about forty locations in Nebraska, Iowa, South Dakota, and Missouri. Ultimately, Rohwer sold the franchise to a Denver-based company with plans for national expansion.

Pepperjax originally offered a menu featuring beef and chicken Phillies, salads, and rice bowls. The company eventually added a bacon add-on while also testing brisket and other meats. A side of specially seasoned French fries and its own brand of sauce (similar to Heinz 57) complete a delicious meal.

As you enter, just walk up to the counter and place your order. Watch them season and cook your meat, and tell them which veggies you'd like to add. You can choose from peppers, onions, mushrooms, and jalapenos. They'll mix the cooked meat and veggies together, melt some cheese over it, and artfully flip it into a toasted hoagie bun, which comes sliding down a conveyor belt—its own little roller-coaster ride. All that's left is to pay at the end of counter, head to a table or booth, and enjoy a tasty meal.

Each Pepperjax location shares Omaha's history through old photographs, both Rohwer family pics and others, including a picture of baseball great Babe Ruth alongside Boys Town founder Father Flanagan.

Top left: The Philly cheesesteak is one of the best in the United States.

Top right: Inside the original Pepperjax location in West Omaha.

Bottom left: Pepperjax also offers salads and rice bowls.

Bottom right: Pepperjax in the Old Market.

2429 South 132nd Street
402-758-9222
pepperjaxgrill.com

HARDY COFFEE

Autumn Pruitt loves baking. That love moved her and husband Luke to return home from Tennessee and open Bliss Bakery inside Aroma Coffee in the Old Market. After opening the bakery in 2010, the couple bought the coffee house two years later.

The couple's savvy for baking and coffee led them to open additional outlets in Benson and at Westroads Mall (they later sold this location). Besides the bakery and coffee houses, the couple roasted coffee beans under the Hardy Coffee brand. Today, all aspects of the business are known as Hardy Coffee, as it helps with brand awareness and growth opportunity.

In early 2018, Hardy Coffee relocated its baking and coffee bean roasting operations to its third location in the Highlander neighborhood, near Thirtieth and Hamilton streets. In a move bringing a popular coffee house to North Omaha, Autumn returned to her roots, having grown up in the area. The staff's love for the Highlander location goes without challenge, as they don't miss carrying heavy bags of coffee beans up the narrow stairway at the Old Market location. Autumn believes the Highlander spot gives people in North Omaha a spot to gather socially or host meetings.

2112 North 30th Street
402-505-9685
hardycoffee.com

"We love Omaha. When I left for college, I never expected to come back, but if we were going to put our heart and soul into a place, then this was the place to do it."

Top left: The Highlander location is the newest spot for Hardy Coffee.

Top right: Hardy Coffee provides beans for several spots around the area.

Bottom left: Mugs and t-shirts are among memorabilia available at the coffee shop.

Bottom right: A pecan roll and latte is a great way to spend time at Hardy Coffee.

TIME OUT CHICKEN

Before it became known as Time Out Chicken, sports stars had an important role in the restaurant building near Thirtieth and Evans streets. Owned by Swanson Corporation—the former Omaha company that brought us the frozen TV dinner—Time Out Foods opened in 1969 as a sit-down restaurant to help develop minority businesses in North Omaha. Featuring local pro athletes Bob Gibson and Bob Boozer as spokesmen, the restaurant even named a burger after them, the "Big Bob."

While the restaurant didn't pan out as designed, a local couple happened to be looking for a place to run. In 1972, Steve Mercer's parents bought Time Out from Swanson. Focusing on its own recipe for fried chicken, the family turned the restaurant into a neighborhood success story.

Helping out at the age of eleven, no one knew that Steve's experience would help him buy the restaurant from his parents after turning twenty-two. His mom, sister, and nephew still help out.

Mercer's devotion to Time Out continues to pay off with it being named as having the best fried chicken in Omaha several times over the nearly four decades he's owned it. He jokes that the secret family recipe puts KFC's to shame. One bite of the well-seasoned bird can convince diners he's right.

While known for its chicken, Time Out Foods' cheeseburger comes in a close second. Order a side of crinkle French fries, baked beans, or coleslaw, grab a strawberry soda, and you have the makings of a delicious meal, and if it's your first time visiting, odds are you'll be back.

North Omaha has seen businesses come and go, but Time Out has long remained a popular spot. Mercer credits the customers with its success. The chicken's recipe, the continuity of service, and its

Top: The fried chicken is amazing at Time Out.

Bottom left: The line forms early at Time Out.

Bottom right: The Time Out street sign is one of the tallest in North Omaha.

location help attract people, and customers reciprocate with repeat business. Mercer rarely finds the need to advertise, as word of mouth has kept him in business.

3518 North 30th Street
402-451-2622
timeoutfoods.com

JIM AND JENNIE'S GREEK VILLAGE

Jim and Jennie Anastasious left their native Greece to spend time with relatives in America. Jim arrived in 1974, while Jennie emigrated seven years later. Planning to live near relatives and work in the country for only a few years, they didn't envision living the rest of their lives away from Greece. Life happens, though, and nearly thirty-five years after opening their restaurant, they wouldn't change a thing.

Jim and Jennie's Greek Village started as a small gyro take-out shop near Ninetieth and Maple streets. Fitting in well as part of a small strip center, the Anastasiouses were content with their sandwich shop, one of only a handful of Greek restaurants in Omaha at the time. A few years later, however, an opportunity to take over the bay next to the shop was too tempting to pass on, so Jim and Jennie's went from a small sandwich shop with a few tables to a sit-down restaurant with lots more space.

Planning wisely, the couple slowly grew the restaurant to become one of Omaha's more popular ethnic dining options. Known for its gyros, customers drool over the gyro platter with large portions of lamb and beef piled high on the plate, lying atop pita bread slathered with a layer of tzatziki sauce and fresh onions and tomatoes topping the entrée. Greek potatoes are also well seasoned and plentiful. The menu offers several other choices as well, with each prepared in Greek style. Of course, no Greek meal is complete without a dessert of baklava or galaktoboureko.

Before opening their restaurant, Jim worked at various eateries, including the former Stockade (which became Millard Roadhouse). As he worked at these restaurants, the thought of running his own place grew from an inkling to turning the key and unlocking the

Top left: Jim Anastasious emigrated from Greece in 1974 and Jennie followed a few years later.

Top right: Jim and Jennie's celebrates its Greek heritage throughout the eatery.

Bottom left: Jim and Jennie's has been open nearly thirty-five years.

Bottom right: People enjoy the gyro combination at Jim and Jennie's.

door to that sandwich shop. As the years pass, Jim reflects fondly upon the restaurant's success. It allowed the couple to raise two children, who became pharmacists. Appreciative of loyal customers, Jim enjoys visiting with them, as several diners are longtime Jim and Jennie's fans.

As the restaurant industry faces challenges with a changing workforce, Jim continues to look forward to taking his spot behind the counter and cooking the day's orders. As for the future? Jim says to ask him in ten years if he's ready to retire.

3026 North 90th Street
402-571-2857
jimandjennies.com

LITHUANIAN BAKERY

Immigrants have flocked to South Omaha for decades. They've come from all over, e.g., Ireland, Germany, Italy, and Latin America. The neighborhood drew Eastern Europeans seeking a better life than their homeland could provide. Omaha's Lithuanian population is probably less than five hundred, but one import remains as the center of the area—the Lithuanian Bakery.

Opened nearly fifty years ago by Vytautas and Stefanija Mackeviscius, the family's torte remains the bakery's most popular menu item. The dessert takes three days to make and consists of eight layers of wafers, each coated with vanilla buttercream and lemon extract, with a layer of apricot in the middle. People covet the torte and arrive early each Saturday—when the torte is available—and are willing to stand in line if necessary.

While the torte dominates the bakery's popularity, the Mackeviscius family also creates delicious bread. Al, who took over the bakery from his parents, creates sourdough rye and country rye. The bakery's "Kommis Brot" is a thinly sliced pumpernickel, which is created in the old-country tradition.

In addition to the bakery, the family runs the Lithuanian Bakery and Café near Seventy-fourth and Pacific streets. The nearly three-decade-old eatery offers the bakery's items as well as a menu featuring European-style bratwursts and Braunschweiger and also American fare. It's a challenge for diners not to enjoy a slice of the torte for dessert.

Lithuanian Bakery
5217 South 33rd Avenue
402-733-3076
lithuanianbakery.biz

Lithuanian Bakery & Café
7427 Pacific Street
lithuanianbakery.biz

Top left: The Lithuanian Bakery is a neighborhood favorite.

Top right: The bakery's entrance greets visitors with handwritten notes.

Bottom left: A mural celebrating Lithuanian history in Omaha is located at the bakery.

Bottom right: The bakery offers a variety of delicious items.

GODFATHER'S PIZZA

From humble beginnings, Godfather's grew into a major player in the pizza world. Willy Theisen opened his first pizza place in 1973. Located next to a bar, Theisen would actually sell his pizza through a hole in the wall between the two businesses. He bought the Godfather's name a year later and created a franchise that would be the top pizza company eight years later.

With the franchise name set, the company quickly grew, becoming number one in sales growth for fast-food chains in 1978. In 1982, Godfather's chain ruled American pizza. Theisen then sold Godfather's to Pillsbury, which owned it until 1990. A local company bought it from Pillsbury, with Herman Cain as the chief executive officer. Cain led the company until 1996. He left as chairman in 2002.

Following a reduction in franchises during Cain's leadership to help increase revenue, Godfather's now has more than five hundred locations in thirty-six states.

Godfather's pizza may be known as much for its mascot as for its food. A sharply dressed man, the Godfather dons a pinstripe suit and fedora. Two local actors are best known for the role since it was introduced in the mid-'70s. Godfather's has had several slogans, including the popular "A pizza you can't refuse" and "Do it!"

Godfather's most popular pizzas include the Classic Combo (featuring pepperoni, beef, sausage, onions, mushrooms, black olives, and mozzarella cheese) and the Taco Pie, with seasoned beef, onion, tomato, lettuce, cheddar cheese, and spicy taco sauce.

3141 North 108th Street
402-493-3833
godfathers.com

Top left: Godfathers' storefront at its Aksarben Village location.

Top right: Godfathers pizza was created in Omaha before becoming popular nationally. Photo provided by Godfathers.

Bottom: Mural of the Godfather.

CATFISH LAKE

They say imitation is the best form of flattery. Don't tell that to Tony Vernon. The longtime owner of Catfish Lake, south of Bellevue, once worked for the master of Omaha's fish dinners, Joe Tess Place. In fact, Catfish Lake sits on land leased from the Fait family, which owns Joe Tess Place in South Omaha.

"I could never be Joe Tess', "Tony says. "I wouldn't want to be. They are special. They are the best."

Still friends with the Faits, Tony has owned Catfish Lake near Offutt Air Force Base since 1986. He remembers catching fish with the Fait brothers as well as working in Tess' kitchen. He learned to cook there and does he know how to cook! Tony creates outstanding fish dishes . . . and then some. While catfish may be the most popular dish on the menu, Vernon creates impressive dinners, including steak and pork tenderloin. In addition to catfish, the restaurant offers walleye and tilapia.

While Tony doesn't believe he's in the same league with Joe Tess Place—he has too much respect for the family to say as much—many customers believe the student has become the master. Catfish Lake strikes the right chord with the food and atmosphere—a casual ambience with a bar and dining room as well as a view of a small lake. The restaurant is packed at night, especially on the weekends.

1006 Cunningham Road
402-292-9963
catfishlake.org

Top: Guests can dine in the lounge or main dining room.

Middle left: Enjoy a full-sized catfish dinner.

Middle right: Catfish logo outside the building.

Bottom: Diners can enjoy a view of the lake during dinner.

STOYSICH HOUSE
OF SAUSAGE

As you walk inside Stoysich House of Sausage on Twenty-fourth Street, you know this is your grandfather's kind of butcher shop. No new-fangled equipment will do here. If you have a side of beef or a deer you want sliced and diced, you bring it to this old-time butcher shop, and Ken Stoysich takes care of it for you. It's been that way since his dad opened the place as a corner grocery store in the early 1960s.

Rudy Stoysich, Ken's father, worked a variety of jobs until one day when wife Rita noticed a corner market for sale. She rode the bus to her job in downtown Omaha and would gaze out the window as the bus rolled past houses and stores along its route. Next thing they knew, the Stoysiches owned a small grocery store. Previously, the building had other businesses, including a barbershop and an auto repair garage.

Running the grocery store, Rudy cut a lot of meat for the neighborhood. As was common back then, Omaha's neighborhoods were segregated by ethnic groups. Several called South Omaha home—Polish, German, and Irish as well as Eastern Europeans. Rudy made a lot of sausage that appealed to the Poles in the area. With a talent for cutting meat and making sausage, the store gained a reputation for its butcher work.

As larger grocery stores started to take hold of the Omaha market, the Stoysiches knew they couldn't compete. It was impossible for them to have four or five varieties of everything like the big stores. So, they transformed their corner market into what they knew best—Stoysich House of Sausage—and the rest, as they say, is history. The shop's reputation as the go-to place for butcher work developed an international following, if you will. Ken prepared bangers—English sausage—for a contingent of British military members at Offutt Air Force Base during the 1970s. They swore they were in London with the taste.

Left: Ken Stoysich learned to be a butcher from his dad.

Top right: Some grocery items can still be purchased at Stoysich.

Bottom right: Stoysich House of Sausage was once a grocery market before transitioning into a butcher shop.

A butcher most of his life, Ken learned the trade from his dad and other butchers at the shop. He cuts almost anything people ask, including deer, elk, and even bear. The one animal that most challenges him is bison, as the animal's size and build require a special process to butcher it. With so many animals to work with, Stoysich House of Sausage offers about one hundred and forty varieties of sausage.

As an advertising gimmick, Ken became the "official" weather guy for a local outdoor activities radio program.

2532 South 24th Street
402-341-7260
stoysich.com

JACOBO'S AUTHENTIC MEXICAN GROCERY AND TORTILLERIA

Today, people drive across town to buy a pint or two of what many call the best salsa in Omaha. Nearly forty-five years ago, Ramon Jacobo rolled the dice and opened a grocery store in South Omaha, believing a market existed for a Hispanic-based grocery store. Moving his family from Chicago back to his native Omaha, Jacobo's opened a month later near Thirtieth and Madison.

With son Carlos helping to manage the store, Jacobo's included a bakery operation in another area of South Omaha. Then, in 1989, thirteen years after opening, the father/son team moved both operations to a central location, as Jacobo's took over a prime corner at Twenty-fourth and L Street. Since then, Jacobo's customer base has transitioned from primarily Hispanic to a mix of diverse cultures.

While lines can form from the deli section to the store's front any day of the week, weekends often see people waiting patiently in a line stretching outside the store into the parking lot. While freshly made burritos, enchiladas, and tamales entice people, it may be the salsa that's the real attraction. Homemade chips and salsa, which Carlos says is a simple and consistent recipe, are so popular that people are willing to drive thirty minutes or longer from the western edge of Omaha just to ensure they have THE thing at pot lucks or family celebrations.

Freshly made tortillas provide a scent that wafts throughout the store. As soon as you enter through the doors, the smell grabs hold of your senses, teasing you to grab a bag during your shopping trip.

Top left: A wide selection of pinatas can be found at Jacobo's.

Top right: Carlos Jacobo manages the store.

Bottom left: Jacobo's has been a staple of South Omaha for decades.

Bottom right: Tortillas are made fresh in-house.

You'll want to pick up ingredients for soft shell tacos, enchiladas, tostadas, or anything else for which you decide to use the tortillas.

Customers often find products exclusively available in a Hispanic-based store. While other supermarkets around Omaha have expanded their international product lines, most people know they'll find what they're looking for at Jacobo's, and if they don't, Carlos will recommend a store that should have it in stock.

4621 South 24th Street
402-733-9009
jacobos.com

BLOCK 16 (page 132)

ZIO'S PIZZERIA (page 136)

FARMERS MARKET (page 50)

PETROW'S (page 56)

WERNER PARK (page 190)

BRONCO'S

Hamburgers
Serv'urself and Save

NOW OPEN
SINCE 1962

BRONCO'S (page 62)

OVER EASY (page 150)

VALA'S PUMPKIN PATCH (page 114)

TED AND WALLY'S (page 144)

KITCHEN TABLE (page 118)

SHIRLEY'S DINER (page 14)

LA CASA PIZZERIA (page 182)

ᴇCREAMERY ICE CREAM & GELATO (page 24)

JACK AND MARY'S RESTAURANT (page 52)

SAKURA BANA

A love for sushi took a man from New York to Omaha, sight unseen, for an opportunity to run his own restaurant. Ikuo "Tony" Asanuma, who relocated to the United States from Japan in 1974, developed his love for sushi in a New York restaurant. He received his first chance to open a sushi eatery when he introduced the concept to Vermont diners, an opportunity which would eventually lead Tony to Omaha.

After three years in Vermont, he wanted to own a restaurant. Then, in 1989, friends in Omaha told him about a two-year-old restaurant for sale. Tony jumped at the opportunity. Before you knew it, he moved to America's heartland, the new owner of Sushi Ichiban. Struggling since it opened, Tony believed he could make the restaurant successful. Offering fresh sushi with good customer service, business improved after about a year. Since then the restaurant has become the face of Japanese dining in Omaha.

In what could have been a dicey move, Tony changed the restaurant's name to Sakura Bana in 2003. Japanese for "Cherry Blossom"—the country's national symbol—the move was in honor of the Vermont restaurant Tony had opened so many years before.

7425 Dodge Street
402-391-5047
sushiomaha.com

Top left: Sakura Bana is Omaha's original sushi bar.

Top right: You can eat at the counter or in the dining room at Sakura Bana.

Bottom: Sushi ranges from mild to spicy with wasabi.

V. MERTZ

One of the first restaurants to open in the Passageway, a beautiful area of Omaha's Old Market, V. Mertz offers a casual, upscale dining experience. Omahans dress eclectically when dining out. You're just as likely to encounter diners wearing suits and beautiful dresses as you are those in a nice top with blue jeans. No matter the attire, at V. Mertz they just want visitors to have a wonderful experience.

Located in a former warehouse, V. Mertz is a key part of the Passageway, a former alleyway converted into dining, art galleries, and boutique shops in the late 1970s, known for its uneven brick floors and walls. The restaurant provides a dimly lit, romantic feel for diners, making it a wonderful site for special events, such as anniversaries, birthdays, or just date night. The restaurant was originally owned by the Mercer family—famous for its Old Market investments—but has seen several new owners through the years.

The restaurant uses locally sourced produce as well as artisan cheeses and sustainably raised meat to create delightful American cuisine, which can be enjoyed as part of a tasting menu or as entrées on small or large plates. Menus change seasonally, so while you may enjoy a salmon belly amuse one visit, your next meal may include lobster or shrimp.

Offering a vast wine selection of about four hundred varieties, servers help choose the perfect drink to complement your dinner.

1022 Howard Street
402-345-8980
facebook.com/vmertzomaha

Left: V. Mertz has a large selection of wines.

Top right: V. Mertz was one of the first restaurants in the Passageway.

Bottom right: Expect upscale service at V. Mertz.

THE JAIPUR

Running the kitchen staff as chef, Gyanendra Bhandari enjoyed providing Omaha with an East Indian dining experience. He created a menu that satisfied the American palate, thus leading to nontraditional Indian cuisine. Open since 1992, Gyanendra and his wife, Smitra, jumped at the opportunity to buy The Jaipur in 2004.

As owners, the couple added fusion to the eatery's menu, creating unique dishes, such as Colorado lamb with garam marsala and fresh vegetables, without sacrificing quality. Dishes associated with Indian restaurants are also available but are slightly different from what you'd find in your more traditional restaurants.

While providing some of the Omaha area's best Indian-style food, The Jaipur also produces outstanding craft beer in their small on-site brewery, among the first craft breweries in Nebraska. The Jalapeno Ale is its most popular beer and goes well with almost any item on the menu. The restaurant also has an enomatic machine, which can fill up to eight bottles of wine.

Located in Rockbrook Village, The Jaipur offers both inside and patio dining. During summer months, patio diners enjoy outdoor concerts presented on weekends.

10922 Elm Street
402-392-7331
jaipurindianfood.com

Left: Gyanendra and Smitra Bhandari took over The Jaipur in 2004. Photo provided The Jaipur.

Top right: The Jaipur has beautiful décor.

Bottom right: Colorado lamb is part of the Indian fusion in which The Jaipur specializes.

The Jaipur annually wins fans' votes as the best Indian restaurant in Omaha.

SINFUL BURGER SPORTS GRILL

A sports bar with a menu based on the seven deadly sins? Only in Nebraska. The tale of Sinful Burger Sports Grill even includes a bit of gambling.

After years of working at Nevada casinos, Jim and Debbie Nearing longed to spend holidays with their family. Known for making unique burgers during family outings they were able to attend, people suggested they should open their own burger place.

Opening the restaurant in Bellevue in 2011, the Nearings sought a theme. Jim's brother mentioned how sinfully good his burgers were; thus, Sinful Burger was born. The restaurateurs based their menu on the deadly sins, with burgers given such names as Gluttony, Envy, Greed, Lust, Pride, Sloth, and Wrath. Each burger includes toppings special to its sins, such as the Sloth's one-third-pound burger with corned beef, Swiss cheese, and homemade Thousand Island dressing. While the Sloth tempts your taste buds with a Philly cheesesteak appeal, the Gluttony tests your ability to enjoy two burger patties topped with cheese and its buns two grilled cheese sandwiches. Bon appetit.

If you prefer a less challenging burger, try the original Sinful Burger, the burger that started it all, as the owners say. Prepared in Jucy Lucy style, a slice of American cheese is melted inside eight ounces of burger delight. It's best to let the burger cool for a time before taking a bite and having the hot cheese ooze its way out of the middle.

If any of the "sin" burgers aren't enough, Sinful Burger challenges customers to try the Goliath—twenty-four ounces of burger slathered in American cheese with tomato, lettuce, and onions between two large pieces of Native American fry bread. If you finish

Top left: Diners enjoy lunch at Sinful Burger in Bellevue.

Top right: Jim and Debbie Nearing opened Sinful Burger after they grew tired of working in Nevada's casino business.

Bottom left: The Wrath Burger is one of the Seven Deadly Sins burgers on the menu. With jalapenos, pepper jack cheese, and chipotle mayo, it's sure to test the senses.

Bottom right: Pictures of those who have tried—and failed—to eat the Goliath Burger.

the entire thing, along with a sinful side of French fries, within an hour, the meal is free, AND you get your picture on the Wall of Fame. Fail and you end up paying more than $30 AND having your picture on the wall of Epic Failures. Choose wisely.

Speaking of the fry bread, Sinful Burger is the only restaurant in the Metro that serves authentic Indian tacos. Debbie, a member of the Rosebud Lakota tribe who grew up on the Pine Ridge reservation in South Dakota, makes each taco fresh to order. Fry bread—a deep-fried flat bread—provides the foundation as traditional taco toppings are built on top.

While it rebounded, Sinful Burger's business was challenged, along with others in its area, in 2016 when major street construction limited access to the restaurant.

4005 Twin Creek Drive
402-933-8727
sinfulburger.com

UPSTREAM BREWING COMPANY

Upstream Brewery chose the perfect spot for Omaha's first brewpub. The building at Eleventh and Jackson has led several lives during its 100+ years. It's been a fire station, a garage, and a theater. Since 1996, Upstream has called the former Firehouse Dinner Theater home.

Fire damaged the location a couple of times, which is sort of ironic since the building served as one of Omaha's fire department stations. Following its public service, the building eventually became home to one of the city's stage theaters. After the Firehouse Theater closed, owners of Spaghetti Works purchased the neighboring building. Once he decided to open a brewpub, Brian Magee bought the building. Magee opened Upstream following more than a decade of experience in the food industry.

After more than two decades, Upstream Brewery remains one of the most popular restaurants and breweries in the city. An Old Market staple, tourists and locals alike flock to the brewpub. Diners view an operational brewery. Upstream produces seven varieties of beer, including the Firehouse red lager. As an homage to Nebraska Cornhusker football history, Upstream named its Bugeater root beer after the school's old nickname.

Diners enjoy Upstream's menu either in the main dining room, upstairs, or outside on the patio, where they can enjoy people watching along with a tasty meal. The flash-fried calamari tossed with banana peppers and cocktail sauce scores as a favorite among diners. The brewpub's entrées range from hand-cut Omaha Steaks to salads to fresh burgers. The pub also serves fresh fish, including salmon.

Top left: Upstream is located in a former Omaha firehouse.

Top right: Downtown Meatloaf is one of the restaurant's favorites.

Bottom left: Fish tacos are menu winners.

Bottom right: The Upstream Brewery creates its local brews on site.

A visit to the Upstream Brewery provides a look into its history as well as some of the best people watching in the Big O.

514 South 11 Street
402-344-0200
upstreambrewing.com

DINKER'S BAR AND GRILL

If you ask a local where to get Omaha's best burger, they'll likely say Dinker's in South Omaha. Once the heart of Omaha's Sheelytown, the sixty-year-old bar, also known as Sheelytown, attracted Omaha's melting pot—Irish immigrants, Polish, and German. The neighborhood has changed over the years, but Dinker's Bar and Grill remains.

Frank Synowiecki, aka Dinker, bought the bar when it was located a couple of buildings down the street. That building remains in the family, and Dinker's remains a popular place to grab one of Omaha's best handmade burgers. "Omaha's Best Burgers" says the sign hanging above the entrance. An Omaha newspaper columnist once said Dinker's had the "best bar burgers" in the city. Frank later translated it to "Omaha's Best Burgers." Regardless, the bar annually challenges as the best in Omaha.

In the old days, factory workers parked themselves on barstools—some were even "reserved," as the same person would regularly sit there—and enjoy a brew after a long shift at the Falstaff brewery or another South Omaha factory. From early morning until closing time, blue-collar workers filled those seats. Hungry, they'd lay a couple of dollars on the counter for a fresh burger prepared on a small cooking plate. Eventually, Dinker's added a kitchen.

The bar had an important role in neighborhood events, such as hosting Santa Claus during the holidays, as well as Easter egg hunts during the spring. Polka bands performed while dancers filled the streets. Dinker's was the center of South Omaha celebrations.

Today, regulars still "own" those barstools, but they share the bar and grill with newcomers, including tourists and families. It may be a bar, but the environment inside Dinker's is family friendly. Television

Top left: The restaurant's popularity ensures a crowd every day.

Top right: A mural celebrating the neighborhood's ethnic heritage is painted the building.

Bottom: Proudly displaying its status as a "best bar burger" in town.

sets showcase Husker and Creighton Bluejays games. Fans attending games in Omaha often grab a pregame meal or a postgame celebration at Dinker's.

2368 South 29th Street
402-342-9742
dinkersbar.com

VALA'S PUMPKIN PATCH

Pumpkins aren't the only thing flying off the shelves at Vala's Pumpkin Patch. After more than three decades, the traditional pumpkin farm expanded to add an apple orchard. On top of it all, the Vala family also enjoys plucking peaches from a small peach orchard.

With thousands of pumpkins sold over a seven-week period, Tim Vala and his family seek to create new ways to continue attracting people to Nebraska's fall version of Disneyland. In the early days, taking a hayrack ride to the fields to pick out a pumpkin was the farm's main attraction. Today, musical entertainment, pig races, and a pumpkin-eating dragon are among the highlights of the Sarpy County pumpkin patch.

Along with the pumpkins and attractions, the 350,000 visitors enjoy about seven thousand handmade chicken pot pies as well as giant turkey legs, footlong corn dogs, and other treats. As they've matured, the Vala daughters—Kirsten, Kayla, and Kelsey—have taken on daily business responsibilities. From social media and group outings to planning the pumpkin patch's food offerings, they spend much of the year planning the season's offerings.

People quickly devour the six thousand pies the kitchen staff bakes during the season. Under head baker Kelsey's guidance, Vala's strives to create new recipes to keep visitors coming back, including a crème brûlée–inspired pie. Along with the popular pumpkin pies, visitors also enjoy apple, peach, and triple berry pies as well as salted caramel apple crunch. Kelsey also created a gluten-friendly apple crisp. She can't ensure it's gluten free because of the preparation area.

Pumpkin patch goers also enjoy a sweet tooth, and the Valas do their best to oblige. Selling more than fifty thousand caramel apples made with apples grown in the orchard, they're easily the most popular item sold at the pumpkin patch. While people also love

Top left: The dining room is packed during pumpkin season.

Top right: Kettle corn is made fresh daily.

Bottom left: Pumpkin is Vala's top-selling pie.

Bottom right: Vala's sells more than fifty thousand caramel apples during its seven-week season.

the fresh kettle corn, which comes in various sized bags, they enjoy freshly made fudge and cookies. In fact, they sell more than three tons of cookies—about 250,000 of the bite-sized chocolate chip treats.

As Vala's looks to the future, the pumpkin patch plans to produce its own apple cider, bottled at an on-site facility near the farm fields.

12102 South 180th Street
402-332-4200
valaspumpkinpatch.com

CUPCAKE ISLAND

There's something about licking the frosting off your favorite cupcake before devouring the sweet treat. At Cupcake Island, they've been creating some of the area's best treats since 2006. With such flavors as Pink Champagne, Strawberry Shortcake, and Devil's Food Among Us, there is no shortage of cupcakes to satisfy your sweet tooth.

Omaha's original cupcake shop opened in 2006, when founders Ed LeFebvre and Shirley Neary sought to create their own style of cupcakes. Ed had worked at a bakery for about twenty-five years and decided he wanted to do cupcakes his way. As the eventual sole owner, he decided it was time to sell the bakery and head off to retirement. So, in early 2018, sisters Melany Dean and Crystal Ryczko realized their dream of owning their own bakery when they bought the shop from Ed. He stayed on for a few months to ensure a seamless transition. It paid off, as no one noticed a change in the cupcakes.

The sisters each have their specialties they'd like to bring to the bakery. Melany is a chocolate connoisseur, while Rachel enjoys making cheesecake. They're slowly easing the additional items to the menu alongside the cupcake mainstays, including the popular Just Say I Do cupcake, as well as daily specials. The bakery also creates cakes for weddings and other celebrations.

Cupcake Island's popularity abounds, as it annually competes for "Best in Omaha" honors as well as being invited to appear on national television programs.

1314 South 119th Street
402-334-6800
cupcakeisland.com

Top left: Cupcake Island bakers also create cakes.

Top right: Cupcake Island is known for its variety.

Bottom left: A confetti cupcake.

Bottom right: Cupcake Island is located in a strip center.

KITCHEN TABLE

Seeking an opportunity to work together, Colin and Jessica Duggan packed up and moved back to Omaha after five years in the San Francisco area. The couple found the perfect building to open Kitchen Table, a restaurant featuring locally sourced food. Situated inside a long, narrow brick-walled downtown building a few blocks west of the Old Market, the Duggans realized their dream of opening the type of restaurant they'd like to eat at.

As a vegetarian, Jessica wanted to create a menu that offered more than just a garden salad. Looking at the menu on a blackboard above the counter, she achieved that goal, with such sandwiches as grilled zucchini jam, featuring hummus, Havarti, dukkah, and tomato balsamic jam on toasted levain bread. Even the grilled cheese is nothing like your grandma's, featuring Havarti with corn and tomato relish on toasted bread.

Kitchen Table caters to more than just vegans and vegetarians, though, as Colin—an avowed carnivore—ensures the menu also includes proteins, such as meatloaf with white cheddar, as well as "the whole bird," a seared chicken breast.

The Duggans offer a quick, healthy alternative to other downtown restaurants, with some menu options less than $10. Kitchen Table has developed relationships with more than forty local farms, with about 90 percent of the menu locally sourced.

While the Duggans call the downtown location home, living in the apartment above the restaurant, they also opened a second location near Fiftieth and Dodge as part of the Filmstream's Dundee Theater.

1415 Farnam Street
402-933-2810
kitchentableomaha.com

Top left: The brick walls add to the laid-back atmosphere at Kitchen Table.

Bottom left: You can add items to your grilled cheese, such as bacon and pickles.

Right: Kitchen Table provides vegetarian alternatives along with meat selections.

ROUND THE BEND STEAKHOUSE

Primarily known for a festival featuring a weekend of eating fried animal testicles, Ashland's Round the Bend Steakhouse offers more than just the private parts of a bull's anatomy.

The Testicle Festival started in 1993 by a previous owner after he had purchased some bull testicles—also known as Rocky Mountain oysters—from a local farmer. He offered the delicacies as part of a festival. About twenty to forty people attended.

Ron and Vickie Olson bought Round the Bend in 1995. Ron wanted to have fun with the festival, so he obtained more food for future festivals. The festival exploded in popularity, soon growing to nearly three hundred people.

The restaurant outgrew its spot in the small community of South Bend, so the owners built a new spot on twenty acres of land atop a hill between South Bend and Ashland. With a ten thousand-square-foot party room added, the Olsons prepared for the Testicle Festival to grow. And grow, it did. Today, almost four thousand people gather on the hill to partake in Rocky Mountain oysters and listen to local bands provide entertainment. The festival, annually hosted on Father's Day weekend, sees about a ton of fried testicles devoured by hungry fans. A distributor works with farmers and ranchers around Nebraska.

Centrally located between Omaha and Lincoln along Interstate 80, Round the Bend attracts diners from all over. Families gather for celebrations, including birthdays, anniversaries, and weddings. Being a family-friendly restaurant resonates with TJ and Tifini Olson,

"We serve quality food at a good price. We think of people like family, and we want them to go home full."

Top left: Round the Bend's Testicle Festival attracts thousands every year.

Top right: Known for its steaks and testicles, Round the Bend also offers great specials, like hamburger steak.

Bottom left: Not sure what to order?

Bottom right: Round the Bend is just around the bend from anywhere.

who took over the restaurant from his parents in 2012. Round the Bend hosts more than one thousand diners each weekend, which is impressive since it's closed on Sundays. The Olsons' faith guides them to use that day for personal reasons and allows employees time to attend church or spend time with family and friends.

While known as the home of the Testicle Festival, the restaurant also offers a full menu, featuring pork tenderloins, chicken-fried steaks, and burgers. The eatery employs an in-house butcher to hand-cut steaks that are then aged forty-five days. They use ground steak to create burgers.

30801 East Park Highway, Ashland
402-944-9974
roundthebendsteakhouse.com

LE BOUILLON

With black cast-iron framed storefronts from the days when vendors sold fruits and vegetables in the Old Market, there's been a Parisian feel near the corner of 11th and Howard for nearly five decades. From the French Café to Le Bouillon, the Old Market offers diners an opportunity to travel to France and sample outstanding fare, all without leaving the confines of Omaha.

Le Bouillon pays homage to its predecessor, the French Café, which was the first restaurant in the Old Market. Occupying its spot at 1017 Howard Street, the French Café took diners on a culinary tour of France for more than four decades. The upscale restaurant eventually succumbed to a changing economy.

Chef Paul Kulik opened Le Bouillon about a year later in the same spot, wanting to provide diners with meals typically found in rural France. With such items as Sweet Pepper Tartines (Castelvetrano olive, braised basque pepper, and white anchovy) for an appetizer, your palate is sure to be enticed to try such entrées as Cassoulet de Castelnaudary (local garlic sausage, duck, pork belly with white beans). Even burgers enjoy a French flair—cantal cheese, mornay sauce, and house quick pickles. Le Bouillon uses locally sourced produce along with meat products, with seafood delivered on a regular basis.

1017 Howard Street
402-502-6816
lebouillonomaha.com

Left: Le Bouillon is the Old Market's French restaurant.

Top right: The restaurant features unique art pieces.

Bottom right: Le Bouillon offers a menu based on French regional foods.

FINICKY FRANK'S

The "Legend of Finicky Frank" drives the menu at the restaurant named after the Ponca Hills character. Based on a neighbor who was apparently choosy over his meal options, Kesa Kenny used the idea when opening Finicky Frank's in the Florence area in 2007.

As you pull into the parking lot, you wouldn't envision a classy restaurant. Located in a parking lot near a gas station and car wash, Finicky Frank's seems out of place, but the location works. The neighborhood features wooded areas alongside traditionally middle-class houses. Once inside, diners are wowed. With fewer than a dozen tables, the restaurant's dining room is spacious, with a bar in the middle.

The restaurant enjoys using locally sourced ingredients as often as possible, with some of the vegetables coming from Kesa's home garden in the Ponca Hills neighborhood. She and husband Brian also look for fresh options during Omaha's farmers market season. Kesa believes using fresh ingredients leads to better-tasting entrées and soups.

A self-taught chef, Kesa also managed the Center Street Café for about eight years before it closed in 2002. It offered sandwiches and soups similar to those found at Finicky Frank's. Finicky Frank's menu also includes handmade onion rings, which Kesa says took several attempts to perfect. The breading envelops the onions and is fried to excellence. Paired with the restaurant's stone ground mustard, it makes a great appetizer or side.

"I believe in good food, fresh, homemade."

Top left: Finicky Frank's strip center location is part of its charm.

Top right: Kesa Kenny is a self-taught chef.

Bottom left: The restaurant offers an intimate dining experience.

Bottom right: Finicky Frank's handmade burgers are amazing.

Casual-style entrées rival those at any high-end restaurant without the high cost. Handmade burgers top the menu along with a tasty pork tenderloin sandwich. Unique sandwiches include a crab cake sandwich as well as a veggie burger. The menu also includes salads and homemade pizzas.

Finicky Frank's opens for lunch and dinner. It's closed on Mondays.

Kesa loves being part of the Florence dining scene alongside several classic eateries. She's an advocate of community development and promotes Florence's attractions, including the Florence Mill and the Mormon Trail Center at Historic Winter Quarters.

9520 Calhoun Road
402-451-5555
finickyfranks.com

OMAHA CULINARY TOURS

A love for food and history led a foodie to create Omaha Culinary Tours to help other foodies discover more about Omaha's culinary scene. Suzanne Allen formed the company with two other partners in 2013.

The company caught on quickly, with tours of Omaha's food districts selling out. Omaha Culinary Tours offers a walking tour of a variety of restaurants in Omaha's popular dining areas, such as the Old Market and Blackstone District. Each tour combines history of the area with the walk, including the Blackstone Hotel as the spot where the Reuben sandwich was invented. Bus tours take foodies around town, sampling classic steakhouse cuisine, as well as visiting some of the city's best pizzerias. A holiday lights-themed tour sells out as soon as tickets go on sale in the summer.

Omaha's reception to OCT filled Suzanne's heart. After moving here in 2000, the thought of creating a food-related tour company grew from her travels, where she would participate in similar adventures. So, she pulled the trigger in 2013 and hasn't looked back.

Today, as the sole owner, she relies on an event manager to handle much of the daily operation. Along with four tour guides, Omaha Culinary Tours now includes private tours for businesses or groups as well as cooking classes and other private events.

As Omaha grows and additional tour companies seek a spot on the culinary map, Suzanne believes Omaha Culinary Tours will continue to be the leader based on the relationships with area businesses and the reputation they've earned with customers.

402-651-0047
omahaculinarytours.com

Top left: Some of Omaha Culinary Tours trips include transportation.

Top right: Sampling food during an Omaha Culinary Tours stop at Big Fred's.

Bottom left: Bryan Peterson samples pizza during a tour.

Bottom right: Guests sample oysters at Plank during an Old Market tour.

PINK POODLE RESTAURANT

Located along America's first transcontinental highway, Pink Poodle has called Crescent home since opening its doors in the 1940s as Bill's Tavern. The owners changed its name to Pink Poodle in 1964. Today, the family-owned restaurant in Crescent, Iowa, continues to serve its famous prime rib.

As US Route 30—aka the Lincoln Highway (named after President Lincoln)—was rerouted away from Crescent, Pink Poodle lost its spot as an attraction along the highway but remained as popular as ever with locals. Fire destroyed the building in the early 1970s, but the owner rebuilt. Today, you're likely to find the two hundred and sixty seats packed on a weekend night. Gone are the old days of dining when men donned suits and women nice dresses; today, you're likely to see T-shirts and blue jeans, but the love for the prime rib, steak, and even seafood remains.

Ownership has remained steady through the years, with little change. With a handful of people owning Pink Poodle, food quality and service has remained consistent. Today, Joe and Jennifer McNeil own the eatery. They bought the restaurant from his mom, a former server who previously bought the Pink Poodle from her boss. Joe worked at the restaurant as a teen, starting out as a busboy.

633 Old Lincoln Highway
712-545-3744
pinkpoodlesteakhouse.com

Top left: Pink Poodle can seat more than two hundred and fifty people.

Top right: The Pink Poodle's sign attracts passers-by on Old Lincoln Highway.

Bottom left: Dolls, stuffed poodle dolls, and other memorabilia fill the restaurant's lobby.

Bottom right: The prime rib at Pink Poodle is among the best in the Midwest.

Explore Pink Poodle Restaurant and you'll see one of the largest doll collections in Iowa.

FLAGSHIP COMMONS

As shopping malls around the United States struggle to remain relevant in an ever-changing economy, Omaha's Westroads sets out to ensure that people continue to visit the fifty-year-old retail center. Teaming with Flagship Restaurant Group, a new style of food court was created. Gone are the fast-food chains that sold burgers and fries. Instead, Flagship Commons created a fast, casual environment offering diners options similar to those of the standard food court but with more upscale menus.

Calling itself an "Uncommon Food Hall," Flagship Commons opened in 2015, offering eight restaurants to order from, including three locally based eateries and five new restaurants. Other than Blatt, customers take their orders and eat in an open common area. That isn't even "common," as it features a fireplace and large-screen televisions. The concept allows parties to choose their own meals—from tacos to sushi—while dining together. The food hall also hosts local singers once a week.

While the food hall targets mall shoppers, it's not unusual for people to meet for dinner and drinks at Flagship Commons. The Blatt offers such an environment, but The Bar in the food hall also offers a place to meet friends and enjoy an evening out.

The three local restaurants are Blatt Beer and Table, Amsterdam Falafel and Kabob, and Aroma's Coffeehouse. Blatt offers a sit-down environment for craft beer and pub food, which is a smaller version of its North Downtown location. While Blatt offers a pub experience, Amsterdam markets itself as "European Street Food," offering sandwiches on flatbread and hummus-based dishes. You can also grab a coffee drink and pastry at Aroma's Coffeehouse.

The five new concepts include Yum Roll, which is an offshoot of downtown-based Blue Sushi. Yum Roll offers fresh sushi and yum-yum bowls (rice-based dishes). If sushi isn't your thing, step next door to Yoshi-Ya Ramen. You can forget your table manners here, as

Top left: The Blatt expanded from downtown to Westroads Mall as part of Flagship Commons.

Top right: Tacos y Mas provides a street vendor style of service.

Bottom left: Flagship Commons isn't your typical food court.

Bottom right: Ramen is a popular menu choice.

everyone is encouraged to slurp their approval with a bowl of ramen. Tonkotsu, a crowd favorite, features pork and chicken mixed with noodles, corn, and an egg in a spicy broth.

Pizza fans enjoy grabbing a slice or two at Weirdough. While you can grab your favorite pizza slice, the eatery offers Butcher pizza, including pepperoni, Italian sausage, and hamburger mixed with mozzarella cheese. Weirdough makes the pizza in squares, a favorite among many Omahans. You can also head south of the border for tacos at Juan Taco, whose spot resembles a food truck. While tacos and quesadillas headline the menu, quality sides include charro beans and green chile rice. If you prefer something lighter and a tad bit healthier, Clever Greens creates salads and wraps to order.

Second floor, Westroads Mall
10000 California Street
402-932-9993
flagshipcommons.com

BLOCK 16

Envisioning their dream restaurant, a young Omaha couple dreamed of a European-style bistro. Instead, Paul and Jessica Urban own one of the most popular and eclectic restaurants in Omaha. Block 16 is as far removed from a European bistro as one can be. Rather than enjoying croissants and a fine wine, Block 16 diners chow down on such creations as Croque Garcon Burger, a one-third-pound burger topped with ham, sunny-side up egg, truffle mayo, and mustard on a ciabatta roll . . . and that's on the conservative side of the menu.

Block 16 grew from a former Greek sandwich shop near 16th and Farnam. Paul and Jessica met while studying at Metropolitan Community College's culinary arts program. The couple brought a deep history of cooking to the relationship. They sought to use it to create a unique restaurant, and when the opportunity to buy the sandwich shop presented itself, they jumped at it. The restaurant even came with Greek food, so the Urbans created dishes using the existing inventory. Then, as it dissipated, they had their own food to replace it. They started creating different dishes, which quickly caught on with the public. So much for the bistro.

While the restaurant offers a core menu (after all, people do need their favorites), Paul and Jessica encourage their team to create daily specials. Paul describes the process as one where chefs at the end of the night look at the remaining food and play around with it to create their midnight meal. Thus, such sandwiches as the Stoner Chikwich are born, with a "flaming hot Cheeto" breaded chicken tender in between two French toast waffles with seasoned jam and more.

While known for its unique sandwiches, Block 16's popularity exploded when TV foodie Alton Brown visited for lunch. The Food Network star shared a photo of the Croque Garcon Burger on Instagram with his nearly five million followers, calling it the best

Left: Block 16 attracts an eclectic dining crowd with its unique menu.
Right: The Croque Garcon Burger has been called the best burger in the country.

burger in the United States. That's all people needed to know. Block 16 was slammed with phone calls and visits from people wanting to try the burger that Alton Brown basically endorsed. Attention settled down after a few months, but they can tell when the episode airs in repeats because the attention booms again.

The couple pride their culinary skills on family heritage. Jessica hails from Canada, with relatives in Europe and Australia. Paul's family calls South Omaha home, with its ethnic melting pot of culinary experiences. Paul's family still owns a century-old garden in the area, which the couple use to raise vegetables for Block 16. The duo believe in supporting a farm-to-table concept as much as possible. They also plan their vacations around food instead of attractions as others do. Instead of making reservations for rides at such places as Disneyland, the Urbans make reservations at restaurants they want to savor.

As Block 16 continues to grow, the couple still dream of opening that European-style bistro in Omaha. Someday.

1611 Farnam Street
402-342-1220
block16omaha.com

LISA'S RADIAL CAFÉ

A longtime fan of Lucille Ball, Lisa Schembri almost turned her café into a shrine to her favorite comedienne. She bought Lisa's Radial Café—she added the "Lisa" after buying the then 62-year-old Radial Café in 2000. Plastering Lucy memorabilia on walls, shelves, and even the women's restroom, some visitors may have thought the restaurant was actually Lucy's.

Lisa, a native-born Californian, owned a restaurant with her husband, Cliff, in the San Francisco area, but, unfortunately, it didn't pan out. Family in Omaha suggested they move here, so Lisa and family packed their bags and headed east. Living in the Benson area, her jobs included waiting tables at the Radial and later at Leo's Diner, when a new owner of Radial let most of the staff go.

In 2000, Lisa seized the opportunity to buy the Radial Café when she learned it was for sale. The restaurant then became Lisa's Radial Café. Serving home-cooked meals and offering impressive customer service—everyone is treated like family—her fan base grew into a loyal following. People stand in line for hours on weekends to enjoy the cooking and camaraderie. Tables are closely bunched, so you may come in as strangers, but the odds are that you'll end up having friendly conversations with people seated near you.

Lisa helped people in the community as well as hired people who needed a job. In one case, she hired a waitress also named Lisa—the "other" Lisa—without an interview or references. After initially telling her she didn't have any openings, Lisa called to tell her to come in the next day all because a customer told Lisa she should hire the "other" Lisa. That was good enough for the restaurateur. The "other" Lisa still serves tables with a smile on her face and a good laugh.

As her affection for Lucille Ball became well known—she even had a dog named Lucy—customers would bring in their own memorabilia of the *I Love Lucy* star.

Left: The line outside Lisa's is usually long on weekends.

Top right: Lisa's family continues to run the restaurant following her passing: daughters Marie and Jennifer, husband Cliff, and son Jacob (not pictured, Meghan).

Middle right: Breakfast at Lisa's.

Bottom right: Lisa Harrison—the "other" Lisa—has been a server for years. She checks on the meal she delivered to Rich and Lynne Laux.

Sadly, Lisa passed away in 2016. Her three daughters—Jennifer, Meghan, and Marie—have kept Lisa's Radial Café open, with Jennifer handling most of the daily operations.

817 North 40th Street
402-551-2176
facebook.com/lisasradialcafe

ZIO'S PIZZERIA

Zio's Pizzeria brings a little slice of New York to the Omaha culinary scene. The restaurant's New York–style pizza has been a favorite among pizza fans since it opened its doors in 1985. With the first location on Dodge Street, Omahans started enjoying pizza by the slice with a bevy of topping options.

Dan and Usha Sherman traveled a lot and fell in love with New York pizza. When the couple decided to open Zio's, they naturally thought New York style was the right style for Omaha. Served on thin crust with a special sauce, it caught on quickly with diners. Zio's expanded to three locations, including the Old Market and near 132nd and Center. The Shermans owned Zio's until 2016, when they sold the chain to Steve Johnson. Johnson and a partner opened a new location near 181st and Wright in 2018.

Zio's remains popular after more than three decades. Diners appreciate ordering pizza by the slice. You can choose your toppings, and the cooks will gladly make it for you. Zio's offers combinations, where customers can order two or three slices with a variety of toppings on each slice. Full pizzas are also available.

The eatery offers more than just pizza. Calzones are a great alternative. Filled with a great amount of cheese—mozzarella, ricotta, feta, or cheddar, depending on the order—mixed with your choice of toppings, such as Italian sausage, green pepper, or black olives, a calzone is a perfect meal. You can also choose specialty calzones.

Dining at Zio's reminds you of a New York pizzeria. Photos of iconic New York buildings and attractions hang on the walls. You can watch your pizza being made as cooks hand roll the pizza dough, tossing it into the air as they create the thin crust. Adding olive oil and then the tomato sauce base, the cooks become artists, adding the toppings and cheese to the pizza. The final product is served on a metal plate, adding to the "New York experience."

Left: Zio's Old Market location is one of the more popular restaurants in the area.

Middle: You can customize pizza by the slice at Zio's.

Right: Zio's décor includes vintage photos of New York life, which works with the New York-style pizza served.

Zio's creates the perfect side salad to go with your pizza order. It's nothing fancy—just lettuce, sliced tomatoes, and onions, topped with breadcrumbs. Locals like to add Dorothy Lynch dressing, a Nebraska original, to give the salad a tangy taste.

The restaurant also serves pasta and hoagies as well as appetizers and dessert.

7834 Dodge Street
402-391-1881
ziospizzeria.com

THE DROVER

A drover may best be known as a cowboy who helped drive cattle herds in the Old West. In Omaha, people herd themselves to The Drover for some of the best steaks in the Midwest. Famous for its whiskey-marinated steaks, the restaurant attracts celebrities and locals.

Opened in 1969 as Cork 'N Cleaver, it became The Drover in 1979. The restaurant's exterior offers a Western saloon appearance. While too young to be considered among Omaha's classic steakhouses, The Drover likely tops the younger generation of steakhouses. Decked in dark wood with a western theme, it's easy to believe you're in the Wild West. The restaurant proudly claims its spot as one of the first restaurants in Omaha to offer a salad bar, beginning in the late 1960s.

Located off the beaten path—its neighbors include a travel agency, hotel, and hospital—The Drover is a destination restaurant. People stand in line during the evening rush for an opportunity to enjoy a mouthwatering dinner. The Drover also annually challenges as the best steakhouse in Omaha, even winning the honor by *Omaha Magazine*'s readers.

2121 South 73rd Street
402-391-7440
droverrestaurant.com

Top left: The restaurant's décor includes a western theme.

Top right: The Drover had one of the first salad bars in Omaha.

Bottom left: Steaks are marinated in whiskey.

Bottom right: The Drover looks like a western saloon as you walk up.

The Drover attracts national media during the College World Series. No one can get enough of the whiskey-marinated steaks.

CLASSIC STEAKHOUSES

Steakhouses in Omaha were once like Starbucks; it seemed there was one on every other corner. That was during the heyday of the Omaha stockyards and Aksarben horse racing. Today, four classic steakhouses remain, with Johnny's Café being the granddaddy of them all. The South Omaha fixture is nearing a century in business, having opened in 1922. Located practically next door to the stockyards, Johnny's founder, Frank Kawa, switched it from being a saloon to a restaurant, where farmers, ranchers, and others could hang out and enjoy a good meal.

Kawa kept the restaurant open 6:00 a.m. to 1:00 a.m., working around stockyard hours. He wanted to be open for farmers delivering cattle to the stockyards during off-hours as well as when businessmen could meet to discuss deals over a good steak and drink. The family, which helped run the café, slept in an upstairs room during downtime. Kawa ran the business until the 1960s, when he turned it over to his sons, Jack and Tom. The third generation of Kawas—Jack's daughters Kari and Sally—took over in the 1990s.

The restaurant was used for a scene in the movie About Schmidt directed by Omaha native Alexander Payne. The Oscar-winning movie mogul enjoys using his hometown in his films. The 2002 movie starred Jack Nicholson and Kathy Bates.

Johnny's Café has remained a popular restaurant through changing times in South Omaha. As the neighborhood has evolved from an Eastern European influence to a more Hispanic flavor, the restaurant has also changed. You'll find such dishes as short ribs on the menu, a popular food in Hispanic cuisine. You'll still find hand-selected, slowly aged steaks, such as New York Strip, Ribeye, and Porterhouse. Hamburger steak, a Nebraska favorite, remains popular with diners.

With Omaha's reputation for great steak, one needs to look no further than Gorat's Steakhouse. Opened in 1944 by Louis and

Left: Steak dinner at Anthony's.

Right: Gorat's is one of the oldest restaurants in Omaha.

Nettie Gorat, the restaurant may be best known as a Warren Buffett hangout. It's common to see the multibillionaire dining at his favorite table alongside friends and business associates, including Bill Gates and Bono. If you wonder, the preferred dish by one of the richest men in the world includes a T-bone steak cooked rare, with a double side of hash browns and a Cherry Coke. While Buffett may be its best-known customer, such celebrities as Liberace routinely dined at Gorat's when the Aksarben Coliseum hosted concerts. Even President Ronald Reagan dined there.

The family owned the restaurant until 2012, when chef Gene Dunn bought it. The restaurateur was involved with several eateries before taking on Gorat's as a sole investment. The décor changed slightly, as the owner wanted it to reflect the 1940s and 1950s. Gorat's maintains local ties to its steaks by serving Omaha Steaks products.

As the longtime anchor restaurant in Little Italy, Cascio's has proudly maintained its position for more than seven decades. Founded by brothers Al and Joe Cascio, the family restaurant began as a steak and pizza house on Tenth Street before devoting itself as a steakhouse. As an Italian steakhouse, Cascio's serves a side of pasta with its entrées. An arsonist destroyed the building in 1978. He was caught twenty years later after bragging about starting the fire. He was convicted and sent to prison.

Reopened at the same spot two years later, Cascio's has continued to be a mainstay in Omaha's steak scene. Continuing its long tradition of using hand-cut, aged steaks, about three thousand people dine there weekly. The restaurant has about thirty-eight thousand square feet of space and regularly hosts special events, such as weddings. Cascio's is currently under its third generation of family ownership, with plans to groom the fourth.

The youngest member of the classic steakhouse group is Anthony's in the Ralston area. Celebrating its fiftieth anniversary in 2018, Anthony's continues to be a family-owned eatery. Known as a great Italian steakhouse, customers enjoy a delicious steak with fresh pasta on the side. Tony Fucinaro, son of Italian immigrants, opened the steakhouse before the area surrounding the restaurant was developed. Seating a little more than one hundred people when it opened, Anthony's can now seat about a thousand people.

With its famous Angus bull mounted on the roof above the main entrance, diners may feel a tinge of guilt . . . until they sit down and order a delicious hand-cut and dry-aged steak. Following an impressive dinner, people can relax in the Ozone Lounge, taking in a variety of groups playing music from the Big Band era to pop rock entertainers.

Anthony's Steakhouse
7220 F Street
402-331-7575
anthonyssteakhouse.com

Gorat's Steakhouse
4917 Center Street
402-551-3733
goratsomaha.com

Cascio's Steak and Pizza House
1620 South 10th Street
402-345-8313
casciossteakhouse.com

Johnny's Café
4702 South 27th Street
402-731-4774
johnnyscafe.com

Top left: Cascio's Steakhouse celebrates its roots in Little Italy.

Top right: Cascio's has one of the largest dining rooms in Omaha.

Bottom left: Johnny's Café is nearly one hundred years old.

Bottom right: Inside Gorat's dining room.

TED AND WALLY'S

Who doesn't love homemade ice cream? Fans of Ted and Wally's certainly do and are willing to stand in line for an opportunity to enjoy some of the best ice cream you'll ever taste. The quality of ice cream is determined by the butterfat percentage. The higher the number, the better the quality. Ted and Wally's ice cream has about 20 percent butterfat, well above the national average. A typical soft serve ice cream only has about 5 percent butterfat.

Ted and Wally's journey to butterfatdom begins in a storefront shop in Lincoln. Opened in Nebraska's capital city in 1984, the owners relocated the store to Omaha's Old Market two years later. In the mid-1990s, a young girl named Jeanne started working at the shop. A few years later her brother, Joe, also became an employee. In 2001, the siblings took over as the owners of Ted and Wally's. Jeanne Ohira handles the artistic side of the business, creating the types of ice cream that become more than three thousand flavors Ted and Wally's offers, while Joe Pittack handles the "non-artistic" chores.

Ted and Wally's unusual location—inside a converted gas station, at the corner of 12th and Jackson—was sort of kismet. With its lease up at its original location on Howard Street, the siblings sought a new spot. The former service station fit their personalities and plans for the store. It proved a great choice, as the location is perfect for attracting customers. They opened a second location in the Benson neighborhood also in an abandoned service station.

Their service station choices may have been subconscious according to Joe. Their grandfather used to build gas stations, while another relative worked for the Environmental Agency and was responsible for removing gasoline tanks that posed a risk to the environment. Joe looks at their stores as a way of recycling former gas stations.

Inside the Old Market location, two century-old ice cream machines sit in the lobby, packed with ice and rock salt, churning

Top left: Ted and Wally's calls a former service station home.

Top right: Ice cream is made daily in century-old machines.

Bottom: Homemade ice cream tastes best, don't you think?

away, producing the day's ice cream. The team begins creating daily flavors about 7:00 a.m., and the process takes about four hours. During the summer, when business booms, they produce twenty to thirty canisters, while winter's business cuts that number in half.

1120 Jackson Street
402-341-5827
tedandwallys.com

THE GREY PLUME

One of Omaha's finest restaurants, The Grey Plume prides itself on being one of the greenest restaurants in the United States. Named as the first four-star Sustainabuild-certified green restaurant, ecological-savvy chef Clayton Chapman ensured his restaurant would be a friend of the environment when he opened in Midtown Crossing in 2010. Using recycled wood and sustainable lighting, nearly everything inside The Grey Plume involves repurposed equipment.

Nominated many times for the coveted James Beard Foundation award for outstanding cuisine, you would expect the chef to be working at an upscale five-star restaurant on one of the coasts. Instead, Chapman sought to share his culinary love with his hometown, and that love is reciprocated. The Grey Plume, which includes his son's middle name of Grey, is one of the best restaurants in Omaha.

The chef's belief in eco-friendliness includes working with local farmers and distributors. From Plum Creek Farm chickens to farm-processed milk from Hartington, The Grey Plume works with nearly twenty Midwest farms. Using locally sourced food to create delicious seasonally based recipes, including in-house churned butter, The Grey Plume's menu often changes because of food availability, but the variety creates an opportunity to sample new dishes.

220 South 31st Avenue, #3101
402-763-4447
thegreyplume.com

Top left: Chef Clayton Chapman is a multi-nominee for the James Beard Award. Photo provided by The Grey Plume.

Top right: Diners enjoying an evening at The Grey Plume. Photo provided by The Grey Plume.

Bottom left: The Grey Plume was the first restaurant to open at Midtown Crossing in 2010.

Bottom right: Staff working in the kitchen. Photo provided by The Grey Plume.

LO SOLE MIO

The story of Lo Sole Mio is one of love. Don and Marie Lo Sole, high school sweethearts, eloped to Pocatello, Idaho, when they were eighteen years old. Fearful of their parents' reaction, the young couple eventually told their parents. After returning to Omaha by train, Marie's parents met them at Union Station. Instead of scolding the young couple, they gave them a basket of goods they'd need to start their lives together.

Two years later, Marie gave birth to the first of their six children. She was twenty-eight when she had the last one. You might think that a couple starting a marriage and young family so early would have the odds against them, but these are the Lo Soles we're talking about. Don, who had worked as a busboy at Gorat's Steakhouse during high school, continued a career in the hospitality field. While tending bar at the Oak Hills Country Club, his chance to cook came one night when the regular chef didn't come in. It was a first step in his culinary career, as Don went on to work as the executive chef at Happy Hollow Country Club. Marie also worked as a hostess.

They eventually wanted to own their own place, so the couple opened Lo Sole's Landmark in downtown Omaha. They ran the business for seven years before their landlord sold the building.

After working for a food distributor, Don still dreamed of his own restaurant. The Lo Soles decided to give it another try, renting the

Our Restaurant Prayer
By Marie Lo Sole

May God bless all who enter here,
For to us they are so dear.
We promise we will fill your bowl,
And pray that God will fill your soul.

Left: The Lo Soles lost their son Dino in an accident in 2013. He loved cooking. Photo provided by Lo Sole Mio.

Right: Chicken parmesan at Lo Sole Mio's.

front of a former grocery store in South Omaha. When creating a menu, Marie believed selling pizza would be the best option. Opening Lo Sole Mio in 1992, the family business took off. They eventually expanded to its current size by adding the remaining bays of the former Foodland store. Today, Lo Sole Mio ranks as an Omaha classic, offering a full-service menu, featuring authentic Italian dishes, such as veal piccata, pasta reggio, and baked lasagna. A dinner includes a bread basket as well as soup or salad with your entrée.

Lo Sole Mio, which based its name on the famous Italian song "O Sole Mio," attracts celebrities when in town. Tony Bennett dined with the Lo Soles before a show at the Orpheum Theater. Baseball's Tommy Lasorda enjoyed meals at the restaurant. Even Nebraska athletics brings its staff to Lo Sole Mio, including Athletic Director Bill Moos and football coach Scott Frost. Photos of celebrities and athletes, many signed, and others showing them palling with the Lo Soles fill a wall near the front door.

The photo that tugs at everyone's heart, though, is a picture of the couple's son Dino. The restaurant's chef—he loved cooking—died in a motorcycle accident in 2013. Marie's heart is full when she talks of the love Dino had for people and their love for him.

3001 South 32nd Avenue
402-345-5656
losolemio.com

OVER EASY

The line outside the attractive building facade tells you the food at Over Easy must be worth the wait. Once seated and as you look around at the other diners in the intimate setting, their meals confirm your suspicions.

When it opened in 2013, Over Easy filled a void for a quality breakfast/lunch restaurant in West Omaha, according to owner Nick Bartholomew.

Realizing his dream of opening Over Easy, Nick enjoys sharing his favorite meal of the day with "friends" from across the city. Breakfast provides some of Nick's favorite childhood memories, with trips to a fast-food restaurant to pick up breakfast for the family. As they drove home, his dad would let the children eat the hash brown rounds out of the bag. It's the little things that we cherish in life.

All grown up, Nick still enjoys his fair share of hash brown rounds, only now the side dish comes with bacon, cheese, and caramelized onions rolled inside. Dipped in balsamic ketchup, the tots provide a tasty treat.

Speaking of the menu, first-time diners must try Over Easy's version of pop tarts. The fluffy pastries are topped with Nutella and seasonal flavors, such as clementine or maple brown sugar.

Breakfast features entrées, such as quiche, biscuits and gravy, and chicken and waffles. Nick bought Localmotive, a one-time Omaha favorite food truck, to get his hands on the recipe for its lust-worthy rounders. The food truck once set up at all hours of the day to sell bite-sized fried balls of dough stuffed with such items as chorizo and scrambled eggs and gravy sausage. Nick believes the treats would do well at pop-up locations or at a smaller version of Over Easy.

While breakfast may be popular with Nick, Over Easy offers a tasty lunch menu, featuring sandwiches, such as the ever popular

Left: Over Easy's dining area.

Top right: Over Easy uses repurposed barn wood as part of its décor.

Bottom right: You might try the homemade pop tarts when dining at Over Easy.

Reuben, along with salads and freshly created soups. Working with seasonal ingredients, the menu may occasionally change.

As you enjoy your meal, take a look around the small eatery. While Over Easy features eleven tables and six seats at the counter, it also treats diners to unique décor. A wall featuring a handwritten menu and message board was made from repurposed barn lumber. The restaurant promotes local businesses with other business' signs. Not to be pigeonholed as a retro restaurant, the opposite wall has a modern, sleek appearance.

If you're in a hurry, Over Easy offers diners a drive-thru option, one of the few sit-down restaurants in Omaha to do so.

16859 Q Street
402-934-2929
overeasyomaha.com

M'S PUB

M's Pub stands as one of the oldest and most popular restaurants in the Old Market. With its casual atmosphere, diners enjoy a unique menu, including such dishes as Lahvosh made with Armenian cracker and Havarti cheese. With eight varieties available, it tops the restaurant's popular menu selections.

With the Old Market being developed by the Mercer family in the late 1960s, the area longed for quality restaurants. While the French Café opened first in the late 1960s, M's Pub, which was named for original owner Mary Vogel, greeted its first customers in 1973. The sandwich shop quickly caught on with its casual atmosphere and quality food.

Situated in the former Central Supply Building, a 2016 fire gutted M's Pub and several other businesses. The restaurant reopened in late 2017. Its renovation nearly matches the original floor plan with its long bar, seating areas, and open kitchen. The restaurant remains as popular today as it was before the fire.

In the nearly forty-five years since it opened, M's Pub has been owned by two families, with Floyd and Kate Mellen buying it in 1979 from Vogel. A few years later Ann Mellen and a partner took over M's Pub from her parents. Today, Mellen in the sole owner.

422 South 11th Street
402-342-2550
mspubomaha.com

Top left: M's Pub looks the same as it did before the fire.

Top right: The Indian lamb satay is delicious.

Bottom left: A look at M's Pub following the 2016 fire. Photo courtesy of Deb Mavis.

Bottom right: M's Pub as it looks following its renovation after the 2016 fire.

M's Pub was one of the first restaurants to open in the refurbished Old Market in the early 1970s.

SAIGON RESTAURANT/ SAIGON SURFACE/ SAIGON BOWL

The Nguyen family brings a unique approach to Vietnamese cuisine in Omaha by offering different menus at not one but three locations. Saigon Restaurant in West Omaha offers traditional fare, whereas downtown's Saigon Surface fuses traditional Vietnamese with a modern twist. Saigon Bowl allows customers to create their own meal in a bowl, targeting a younger crowd.

The story begins when Hien Nguyen arrived in the United States as a refugee following the Vietnam War, which ended in the mid-1970s. After wife Be Lam arrived, the couple opened Saigon Restaurant in 1997. Saigon offers Omahans a taste of their homeland with staples, such as pho, which is a soup broth featuring rice noodles and protein, and Vietnamese-style chicken wings. Saigon also serves entrées, such as pork chops and chicken. Most diners enjoy the pho with chicken, shrimp, and other protein items.

While Saigon's décor offers a style that draws on many Asian cultures, especially Vietnamese, daughter Ngoc's Saigon Surface showcases a sleek, modern look. Diners view menu options on tablets at each table or booth. Saigon Bowl's décor at Aksarben Village is contemporary and more representative of health-conscious customers, where they can create their own soup bowls.

Top left: Authentic pho at Saigon Restaurant.

Top right: Saigon Restaurant showcases Asian heritage with its décor.

Bottom left: Diners can view pictures of their menu options at downtown's Saigon Surface.

Bottom right: Located at the Bel-Air Plaza, Saigon Restaurant has been popular with locals since opening.

Saigon Restaurant
12100 West Center Road
402-697-7000
facebook.com/SaigonOmaha

Saigon Surface
324 South 14th Street
402-614-4496
saigonsurface.com

Saigon Bowl
6307 Center Street
402-884-8770
saigonsurfacebowl.com

STELLA'S

Ever been hungry enough to down six burger patties, twelve pieces of bacon, six slices of cheese, and six fried eggs between a bun? Wait. Don't answer yet. Let's top it off with lettuce, tomato, fried onions, jalapenos, peanut butter, and pickles. Add a side of French fries. How about now? If you eat it in forty-five minutes, it's free, and you get your picture put on a wall of fame along with taking home a T-shirt of your accomplishment.

Hundreds of people have tried—and hundreds have failed—to eat the Stellanator at Stella's in Bellevue. Actually, only about a dozen people have succeeded; among them is Molly Schuyler, a professional competitive eater (she did it twice, once in less than four minutes). Those who fail have their pictures put on a wall of shame.

Stella's is one of those places you have to visit when in town because you just have to have a greasy burger. Be prepared to stand in line for a while, as people love to enjoy Stella's burgers along with a side of fries or onion rings.

You can customize your burger to satisfy your cravings. A popular combination includes peanut butter and bacon atop the burger. The taste of sweet and salty rocket off the taste buds. Some people prefer a fried egg on their burger, but however you want yours, Stella's can satisfy.

Forget plates and silverware. Stella's doesn't believe in them. Lay napkins on the table and get your fingers messy in eating some of the best food you will ever taste.

How did Stella's become THE place for a burger in the Metro? It all starts with a young woman named Estelle Francois Sullivan Tobler, who, along with husband, Al Sullivan, opened a service station named Francois and Sullivan in 1936. Later, they added a bar, becoming Bellevue's first tavern owners.

Left: Burgers are custom made. Peanut butter and bacon add a unique combination.

Top right: The Stellanator Hall of Fame—more than six hundred have tried, but only twenty have succeeded.

Bottom right: Stella's has been considered the home of Omaha's best burger for years.

With Francois and Sullivan enjoying a successful run, Estelle wanted a larger place for her tavern customers, so the couple bought a second location in 1936. Sadly, Al passed away that year, leaving Estelle alone with their young family.

Undaunted, Estelle trekked on, buying the current location in 1949. She then moved the tavern building to the spot—a former dairy farm—and changed its name to Stella's. She ran the restaurant for another twenty-five years until suffering a stroke. Her son, Al Jr., and his wife took over Stella's and ran it for another thirty-three years. With her uncle and aunt deciding to retire, Stephanie Francois took over Stella's in 2007.

106 South Galvin Road
402-291-6088
stellasbarandgrill.com

TAQUERIA EL REY

Tacos. Burritos. This is how Rey Nava decided to make a living. Having worked in the restaurant industry for more than two decades, Rey saw a market for Mexican food in South Omaha while walking along Twenty-fourth Street with his wife. So, in the summer of 2004, Taqueria el Rey was born as a food truck, serving tacos, burritos, and sopa along South Omaha's main business corridor.

Within four months after launching the food truck, word of mouth made the food truck a popular dining option. Rey looked for a spot where they could prepare the food and tortillas. A former pizza place at Twenty-fourth and Q was available, so he leased it. Less than three years later, Rey owned the building, which is now the main location for Taqueria el Rey, which serves breakfast, lunch, and dinner. Rey believes the restaurant, on the south end of the business district, sits at the best possible spot because of the traffic that passes through the area. Rey also has four food trucks, including one in Lincoln, and owns a second restaurant in Lincoln. The Omaha restaurant uses two cars to deliver meals, and Rey even helps out as a delivery driver.

With tacos being the most popular item on its menu, the restaurant produces about seven thousand weekly. Rey and his kitchen staff also prepare handmade tortillas daily, beginning about 6:30 a.m. The staff, consisting of family and friends, have been together for most of the time since Taqueria el Rey opened its doors in 2004.

5201 South 24th Street
402-502-0674
taqueriaelreydeomaha.com

Top left: You can dine in, order drive-thru, or have food delivered from Taqueria el Rey.

Top right: Breakfast is a great meal at Taqueria el Rey.

Bottom left: Lunch combos offer a variety at the South Omaha restaurant.

Bottom right: Taqueria el Rey has called South Omaha home since 2004.

CALIFORNIA TACOS
AND MORE

L ocated in the building his grandfather built in 1914, Brad Bogard has served tacos his way since 1995. Once home to Bogard Pharmacy, the building at the corner of Thirty-second and California streets ranks as one of the best places in Omaha to get a taco. California Tacos and More has attracted everyone from starving college students to business executives over the past two decades.

A must-see among local restaurants, California Tacos calls Midtown home. Known for its fried, puffy taco shells, the restaurant serves up its namesake taco with a ton of hamburger, lettuce, cheese, and tomatoes. It takes a fork to eat it right. Served with delicious sides, such as refried beans and Mexican rice, it's a challenge to leave California Tacos without feeling satisfied and full.

Centrally located, business professionals trek over from their offices and stand in line alongside students from Creighton University and the University of Nebraska-Omaha. California Tacos sits in an eclectic neighborhood with older businesses as well as residential homes. People also enjoy grabbing a drink from the Margarita machine.

After standing in line, which can often extend outside and around the corner, diners place their order. The order is hooked to a clothesline and pushed to the kitchen. Tippers are recognized with a cowbell being rung when they put money in the tip can.

California Tacos and More's popularity has landed it on national television network programs, such as Food Network's *Diners, Drive-Ins and Dives.*

3235 California Street
402-342-0212
californiatacosandmore.com

Top left: California Tacos and More's Mexican theme highlights a visit to the restaurant.

Top right: A California taco with sides is more than filling.

Middle left: Time for a taco?

Bottom left: The line to order moves along quickly.

Bottom right: California Tacos is located inside a former pharmacy.

OJ'S CAFÉ

OJ Vlcek saw an old shack. She had to be talked into opening a Mexican restaurant on the north edge of Omaha just a few feet from the Missouri River and off Interstate 680. Wanting to run her own restaurant, she rolled the dice and came up a winner when she opened OJ's Café in 1976. Realizing a longtime dream, OJ turned the restaurant into one of Omaha's first authentic Mexican eateries.

Struggling for the first five years, she continued to put in a lot of hard work to make her dream a reality. Eventually, OJ's Café caught on with locals, and she's been serving some of the best cottage cheese-filled enchiladas and tacos in the Metro for more than forty years. She believes customers appreciate having fresh Mexican entrées made from scratch.

Resembling a Western saloon outside, the restaurant grew from a "shack," doubling its size through expansion.

It's the only restaurant on her street, next to the Florence Mill. With area attractions nearby, including the Mormon Winter Headquarters museum, OJ's attracts its fair share of new customers. While she enjoys meeting new people, OJ appreciates her longtime customers, some of whom dine there several times a week. It attracts people from all backgrounds, blue- and white-collar workers, Florence residents, and West Omahans. Being a five-minute drive from the Nebraska-Iowa border, West Omaha customers show a commitment to OJ's by sometimes driving thirty minutes to enjoy the homemade Mexican entrées.

> "I still enjoy cooking. I don't mind turning that key in the door in the mornings."

Top left: OJ has expanded the restaurant since opening in 1976.

Top right: OJ's Café has the look of a western saloon.

Bottom left: A model of OJ's Café is part of the décor.

Bottom right: OJ's cottage cheese-filled enchiladas are a favorite among diners.

Having run the diner since it opened, OJ doesn't plan to retire any time soon. Still enjoying cooking for others, OJ knows when the time comes her son will be ready to take over. He and his wife currently help with the restaurant.

OJ's Café joins a growing number of restaurants rejuvenating the food scene in the Florence area. Besides OJ's Mexican food, diners also enjoy sampling Italian and American fare in the neighborhood.

9201 North 30th Street
402-451-3266
ojscafeomaha.com

TRINI'S MEXICAN RESTAURANT

As the first restaurant to open in the Old Market's Passageway, Trini's grew into a favorite among diners interested in a quality authentic Mexican dinner. The Passageway, one of Omaha's most photographed areas, turned a former alleyway into a dining and retail attraction.

Trini's opened in 1978, and Rich Anderson came aboard as a server a few years later. He went on to manage the restaurant before heading off to start his own businesses, including The Nook, a boutique a short walk from Trini's. His love for Trini's solidified his decision to buy the restaurant in 2010.

Making only a few minor menu changes, Rich sought to keep its offerings and service as consistent as possible. That consistency paid off, as Rich enjoys visiting with regulars during their customary multiday excursions to Trini's. The restaurant is perfect for date nights or dinner before downtown concerts or sporting events.

Popular with locals and visitors, Trini's lists fish tacos among its most popular menu items. A chicken and portabella enchilada also scores well with diners. Trini's offers a nice selection of combination plates, including Mexican traditions, such as tacos and burritos, served with refried or black beans and Spanish rice.

1020 Howard Street
402-346-8400
trinisoldmarket.com

Top left: Chips and queso dip are a great way to start your meal at Trini's.

Top right: The restaurant at the Passageway provides a romantic, dimly lit feel to Mexican dining.

Bottom left: Trini's was the first restaurant to open in the Passageway.

Bottom right: Fish tacos are among diners' favorites at Trini's.

CRESCENT MOON ALE HOUSE

Did you know that Omaha gave birth to the Reuben sandwich? It's believed that a chef at the historic Blackstone Hotel created the corned beef sandwich upon the request of Reuben Kulakofsky, who was playing a hand of poker. The chef added sauerkraut and cheese on a toasted sandwich, and voilà, the Reuben was born! Omahans remain staunch in their defense of being the home of the Reuben despite other stories that the sandwich may have been created at a New York deli.

Crescent Moon Ale House proudly ties the sandwich to its menu. After buying the bar and grill in 1996, Bill Baburek sought to create a menu that would attract diners in addition to beer lovers. Since the Blackstone was located across the street from the bar, he thought it was the perfect connection. Today, the menu includes the Blackstone Reuben sandwich as well as Reuben egg rolls among its options. Omaha Steaks provides the corned beef for the restaurant. Crescent Moon also hosts an annual Reubenfest, featuring all things Reuben—sandwiches, egg rolls, soup, and nachos. The early bird definitely gets the Reuben treat during the weeklong celebration, as the bar and grill sell out quickly.

The bar and grill provide a neighborhood feel while dining. The staff is friendly and recognizes regular customers. The bar offers a comfortable setting with a dining area as well as the bar counter and pool tables. An old-fashioned German bier hall—the Huber-Haus—is located in the basement. Bill owns a small liquor store next door. He also owns Infusion craft brewery in the Benson area.

3578 Farnam Street
402-345-1708
beercornerusa.com/crescentmoon

Top left: Reuben egg rolls are a top seller at Crescent Moon.

Top right: Ready to enter a cosmic bar?

Middle left: A look at the bar.

Bottom left: Crescent Moon's Reuben sandwich has annually been voted the best in Omaha.

Bottom right: Crescent Moon's basement is home to Huber-Haus German Bier Hall.

OMAHA STEAKS INTERNATIONAL

Known internationally for its high-quality steaks, the tradition began more than a century ago when two Latvian brothers emigrated to the United States, settling in Omaha. After working for a variety of butcher shops, JJ and BA Simon bought a building for their own butcher business. Opening as Table Supply Meat Company (they inserted Meat in front of Company to change the building's name), the brothers sold meat to grocers and restaurants.

When BA's son Lester joined the company in 1929 during the Great Depression, the company took off. Signing a deal with Union Pacific to serve steaks in their passenger cars proved profitable, as people enjoyed "Omaha Steaks" on their travels from Omaha to Los Angeles. As word spread about the steaks, restaurants around the country wanted Omaha Steaks.

Then, in 1952, Lester led the company's foray into the mail order business, with magazine ads and mail order flyers. As the company improved vacuum sealing and packaging, sending steaks through the mail grew. The company created its first catalog in 1963.

Table Supply Meat Company changed its name to Omaha Steaks International in 1966, the same year the company moved from its downtown location to a new corporate facility near 96th and J streets. Omaha Steaks took off from there. Opening its call center in the 1970s, the company also opened its first brick-and-mortar stores. In 1990, Omaha Steaks sold steaks online through a partner before creating its own website in 1995.

Today, Omaha Steaks sells more than $450,000,000 annually in food products. Steaks, fish, and other products are delivered around the world. With about eighty stores in twenty-eight states, Omaha Steaks ensures it maintains its position as the "world's butcher."

Top left: A sample of Omaha Steaks.

Top right: Omaha Steaks has about eighty stores located around the country. Photo provided by Omaha Steaks.

Bottom left: Todd Simon is a fifth-generation owner and the face of Omaha Steaks. Photo provided by Omaha Steaks.

Bottom right: Omaha Steaks headquarters. Photo provided by Omaha Steaks.

Company leaders realize Omaha Steaks must continue to improve and diversify to remain relevant in an ever-changing marketplace. Besides its hand-cut, twenty-one-day aged steaks, the company has added fresh seafood as well as slow cooker and skillet meals to its inventory.

While it's easy to think of Omaha Steaks during holiday season and for special occasions, the company is actually busy year-round. During the Christmas holiday season, however, Omaha Steaks typically triples its workforce to meet customer needs.

10909 John Galt Boulevard
402-597-3000
omahasteaks.com

JUNIOR'S FORGOT STORE BAR & GRILL

In the early 1900s, people on horseback stopped at the store between north Omaha and Fort Calhoun, tying their horses to a post or pulling their buggy near the front door. The Forgot Store supposedly got its name because it was thought to be the last place to buy things farmers may have forgotten during their trip to Omaha. Later, as the city improved the road for automobile traffic, cars pulled off so that the driver could gas up or pick up forgotten items.

The building has served different roles since being built in 1925. From a general store to a flophouse to a bar and grill, at least six owners called the Forgot Store theirs. Today, Junior Mathiesen owns the bar and grill, renamed Junior's Forgot Store. Junior ran the former Anchor Inn for about twenty-five years. The 2011 flood forced the bar and grill to relocate from its Missouri River location. After a few years near Ralston, he closed because it never felt the same as it did along the river.

Looking for a new restaurant venture, Junior took over the Forgot Store. Once a hub for motorcycle groups on poker runs and locals taking in fall colors along Calhoun Road, the Forgot Store fell on rough times. After he took over, Junior renovated the interior with new flooring as well as a kitchen makeover. Still popular with motorcycle groups, Junior's Forgot Store also welcomed back locals looking for a nice place to enjoy a meal and drink.

Junior's burgers, pizzas, and wings score as popular items on the menu.

While the Forgot Store enjoys a history dating back to the days of the buggy and Model T Ford, its real claim to fame may be that it's the site of the song "Convoy." World-famous composer and musician Chip Davis, a longtime Omahan, wrote the song along with Bill

Top left: Local musician Chip Davis penned his hit song "Convoy" at the bar and a copy of the Gold Record hangs there.

Top right: Junior renovated the bar and grill when he took it over in early 2018.

Bottom left: The Forgot Store was once a general store for people traveling from Omaha.

Bottom right: The meat lovers pizza at the Forgot Store is on level with local pizzerias.

Fries, aka C.W. McCall, while sitting at a table in the bar. Davis donated a copy of his Gold Record plaque to the Forgot Store, where it still hangs on a wall.

11909 Calhoun Road
402-451-0291
facebook.com/juniorsforgotstore

TASTE OF OMAHA

Thousands of people flock to Omaha's riverfront for a three-day festival celebrating a Taste of Omaha. Dozens of local vendors, from restaurants to food trucks, offer scaled-down versions of their regular menus. Running the gamut from Mexican to Italian and all things in-between festivalgoers sample delicious sandwiches, entrées, sides, and more. Chowing down on a Runza, a slice of pizza, or a corn cob on a stick, food fans will find Taste of Omaha has a little something for everyone.

The celebration, which runs from the Heartland of America Park to Lewis and Clark Landing, features entertainment and merchants selling wares, such as jewelry and hot tubs. Food may be the major draw, but stages are located throughout the event, featuring local and national music acts. Running late into the night, visitors definitely get their fill of food and fun.

While the festival continues to grow annually, it remains a family-friendly event, offering attractions that appeal to all ages, including carnival rides, magic acts, and fire-spinning dancers.

Held the first weekend of June, Taste of Omaha traditionally kicks off the city's summer festival season, which includes an event weekly through mid-July.

7015 Spring Street
402-346-8003
showofficeonline.com/TasteHome

Top left: Thousands of people participate in Taste of Omaha over a three-day weekend.

Middle left: Food trucks are among the food vendors at the festival.

Bottom left: Concerts and rides are a big part of Taste of Omaha along the riverfront.

Right: Fire eaters acts using fire as part of their performance.

LE VOLTAIRE RESTAURANT AND LE PETIT BAKERY

West Omaha proved the perfect spot for Chef Cedric Fichepain to open Le Voltaire and his bakery Le Petit. Being located in a strip center may not seem like an ideal spot for a trendy French restaurant, but Le Voltaire is far from a trendy French restaurant. He could have opened a restaurant in the Old Market or any other highly visible spot in Omaha, but Chef Cedric believed the spot at Pepperwood Village would work.

The French-born chef came to the United States in 1997, two years after marrying Fremont native Desarae Mueller. Having worked in a variety of restaurants, including the former Farucci's Bistro, the chef felt ready for his own place, and in 2001 he and Desarae selected Le Voltaire to be the eatery.

While not initially sure how receptive people would be of a French restaurant in West Omaha, as the city's population moved westward, his restaurant was perfectly located for a growing customer base. While some would consider Le Voltaire upscale—the ambience definitely resembles a classic French eatery—prices won't bust anyone's budget.

Since it's a French restaurant, the menu rivals anything you may find at a restaurant along the Champs-Élysées in Paris. The menu changes seasonally, but staples remain available, including Boeuf Bourguignon (beef stew simmered in red wine, carrots, mushrooms, and onions) and Cassoulet de Tarbes (a duck confit, garlic sauce, bacon, and white beans).

Chef Cedric also owns Le Petit bakery next door. The bakery offers croissants made with pure butter, handmade eclairs, and macarons, among the many baked sweets and breads. Add a cup of rich coffee

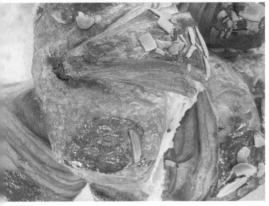

Top left: Le Voltaire offers intimate dining.

Top right: Duck confit is a must at Le Voltaire.

Bottom left: Le Petit's croissant challenges any you would find in a Parisian bakery.

Bottom right: Le Voltaire and Le Petit bakery are located next to each other.

and enjoy the treat at one of the outdoor tables and feel like you're at a Parisian sidewalk café.

Additionally, Chef Cedric serves as the honorary French Consul for Nebraska, South Dakota, and North Dakota. A noted author, he has cowritten *20 Percent and Counting*, following the daily life of a server, and *Fowl to the Bone*, a murder mystery

569 North 155th Plaza
402-934-9374
levoltaireomaha.com

DUNDEE DELL

With about seven hundred bottles of scotch filling up a wall behind the bar, one may think Dundee Dell is a bar for gentlemen to sip an aged scotch and discuss the day's events. Nothing could be further from the truth. The bar and grill—really, it's a pub—in the Dundee neighborhood courts "regular" folks, who may enjoy a drink alongside their fish and chips.

Originally named Dundee Delicatessen, the restaurant opened in 1934. Later, it became Dundee Dell and called the corner near Fiftieth and Dodge home for decades, but with commercial development looming in the early 2000s, the owner relocated to Underwood Avenue, where it continues to serve as one of the most popular spots in Omaha to eat fish. Known for its fish and chips, Dundee Dell offers a fun experience for people to meet with friends or family for a nice meal or evening out.

With four owners during its lifetime—the first three having the eatery for twenty-seven years each—Dundee Dell's consistency remains a popular attraction with diners. Menu items come and go, but its core remains in place, led by the fish and chips, which are served in heated aluminum bags.

Outside the building on Underwood Avenue hangs a plaque recognizing the time Omaha was attacked during World War II. A balloon-carried bomb exploded over the Dundee neighborhood, resulting in the farthest inland attack on the United States during the war.

5007 Underwood Avenue
402-553-9501
dundeedell.com

Top left: Dundee Dell has about 700 varieties of scotch.

Top right: Artwork at Dundee Dell.

Bottom left: The Dell is known for its fish and chips.

Bottom right: Dundee Dell prides itself as a pub.

BIG MAMA'S KITCHEN

Patricia Barron—aka Big Mama—loved cooking. The retired phone company manager wanted to open her own restaurant in North Omaha, but she couldn't find any of the city's banks willing to work with her. She was too nice to say it was an age issue.

Big Mama operated a catering business out of her home for a while. Seeking to open a family-style eatery, Big Mama looked for a place to prepare her favorites. Without a place to call home, Big Mama refused to give up looking. Then, almost miraculously, she found the spot—the cafeteria at the former Nebraska School for the Deaf.

With equipment in place, including pots, pans, tables, and chairs, all Big Mama needed was her recipes and a staff. Opening its doors in 2007, Big Mama's popularity surged with the Omaha dining scene. People love the homestyle cooking. Big Mama, herself, was a draw. With a big personality and love for everyone, Big Mama loved cooking for people.

While her culinary career started late in life, Big Mama enjoyed a lifelong love of cooking. She recalled during her childhood that her family would fry chicken for sandwiches when traveling to the South because restaurants refused to serve African-Americans. Following a stint in the Navy, she fulfilled her love of cooking by enrolling in a culinary arts program at MCC while working full-time at the local telecom company, where she stayed until she retired.

Big Mama earned a great reputation. She found herself the darling of national television programs, such as Food Network's *Diners, Drive-Ins and Dives* and Travel Channel's *101 Tastiest Places to Chow Down*. Sundance Network also featured the restaurant on *Ludo Bites America*. Big Mama and her family filmed a reality show pilot, but it wasn't picked up because she thought there wasn't enough drama.

Top left: Big Mama's is known for its oven-fried chicken.

Right: Diners are greeted by a reminder to have a slice of sweet potato pie.

Bottom left: Big Mama appeared on several cooking shows, including the Food Network, where she met Guy Fieri.

Big Mama passed away in early 2018 at the age of seventy-six. Her three daughters honored her request to continue running the restaurant. While she may be gone, the sisters keep her memory alive at the eatery.

Big Mama's daughters plan to move the restaurant—best known for its oven-fried chicken—to the Highlander Accelerator Building near Thirtieth and Parker streets in 2019.

3223 North 45th Street
402-455-6262
bigmamaskitchen.com

ROMEO'S MEXICAN FOOD AND PIZZA

Where do you go when someone in your group wants Mexican food while others want pizza? In Omaha, Romeo's would be the perfect spot to satisfy both appetites. When the original location opened at 90th and Blondo in 1976, the plan was for Romeo's to be a pizza place. Based on the former Casa De Reyes restaurant, the Mexican food concept remained popular, so the owners decided to go with both menu options. They even named the No. 1 combo plate after Casa De Reyes, which features one enchilada, taco and burrito, alongside beans and rice.

In addition to excellent Mexican food, diners can enjoy a variety of pizza options featuring the restaurant's special sauce. Pizzas come in three sizes on thick dough—personal size at eight inches, thirteen inches, or a large at sixteen inches. The North of the Border menu also includes hamburgers and ham and cheese sandwiches.

With five locations scattered around the Metro area, each Romeo's has its own unique décor. From posters featuring Southwest Native American tribes and celebrations to TV screens for people to watch a sporting event during their visit, Romeo's has developed a loyal following through the years.

2395 No. 90th Street
402-391-8870
romeosomaha.com

Top left: Romeo's location near Ralston.

Top right: Chips and cheese queso are a must at Romeo's.

Bottom left: Casa de Reyes combination is a tribute to the former Mexican restaurant.

Bottom right: Romeo's has five restaurants around Omaha.

LA CASA PIZZARIA

You know you're doing something right when people still enjoy dining at your restaurant after nearly seven decades. La Casa Pizzaria opened its doors in 1953, with founder Joe Patane at the helm. As one of the first restaurants in Omaha to offer pizza, La Casa's Neapolitan-style pies immediately caught on with diners.

On opening day, the restaurant ran out of food. After four years, La Casa expanded, more than doubling the size of the original building. As is the case with many classic Omaha restaurants, La Casa enjoys a true family environment, with Joe's grandchildren Nicole Jesse and Joel Hahn managing it. Today, Joel's son Brandon assists in managing the restaurant, introducing a fourth generation to the family business. Anthony Vacanti, a cousin, operates other La Casa locations.

The grandchildren started working in the family business as children. Nicole recalls helping her grandma roll dough as a youngster and started as a hostess when she was in high school.

Known for its unique flavor, La Casa's pizza rates among the best in Omaha. Using Romano as the primary cheese and its own special sauce, La Casa creates a unique-tasting pizza. Still baked in square pans, the tradition started when Joe opened the restaurant because bakeries used them during the 1950s. They used a gas-fed shelf oven to bake the pizzas. With New York–style pizza known for its pepperoni, Joe wanted to be different, so he topped theirs with hamburger. Living in the middle of beef country, how could he be wrong?

As one of the first restaurants in Omaha to list pizza on its menu, the staple now shares the menu with calzones and all types of pasta dishes, including lasagna, fettuccine, spaghetti, and mostaccioli. Topped with either marinara or spicy rosa sauce, the pasta tastes amazing, especially when adding a couple of meatballs.

Top left: La Casa's customers are treated like family.

Bottom left: Homemade sausage and peppers at La Casa.

Right: Romano cheese brings a different flavor to La Casa's pizza.

La Casa's owners believe in following their grandfather's advice—always be moving forward; otherwise, you're moving backwards. In addition to serving diners in the restaurant, customers can order takeout as well as order online for pizzas to be shipped out of town. They also cater parties. La Casa's food truck has been patrolling the streets of Omaha since 2013.

4432 Leavenworth Street
402-556-6464
lacasapizzaria.net

SADDLE CREEK BREAKFAST CLUB

A desire to be home at night led to one of Omaha's newest and hippest restaurant concepts. Long known as a city with great breakfast options, Chef Chase Thomsen thought he could take breakfast, his favorite meal of the day, to a new level. Saddle Creek Breakfast Club opened in 2017 and immediately started drawing crowds.

Chef Chase and his wife, Nikki, had a baby in 2017. As many parents do, he wished he had more time to spend with his young family. The opportunity to open a breakfast/lunch eatery and be home at night was too good to pass up. Using his extensive kitchen experience, he created the Saddle Creek Breakfast Club, which is open from 7:00 a.m. to 2:00 p.m. daily (closed Mondays). The schedule allows him to be home during the evening, living a somewhat normal life for someone in the food industry.

Situated in classic Midtown Omaha, Saddle Creek Breakfast Club calls a former service station home. With two small dining rooms available, the early bird gets the best seats here. During the week, visitors can get a table fairly quickly. Weekend diners can expect a wait, often with a line outside the small lobby, but the staff offers a hot cup of coffee while you wait, supplied by Amateur Coffee, a local roaster.

Once seated, the menu makes the wait worthwhile. With unique offerings, such as banana pancakes with crushed peanuts, honey, and topped with a peanut butter whip, Saddle Creek Breakfast Club has earned a reputation as a place to try new takes on standard breakfast fare. Farm-fresh eggs take front and center on the menu, featured on such meals as the Saddle Creek Standard, paired with hash browns

Top left: Saddle Creek Breakfast Club offers breakfast and lunch.

Top right: Farm fresh eggs add a unique taste to breakfast.

Bottom left: The SCBC logo brightens the day of passers-by.

Bottom right: Located inside a former gas station, Saddle Creek Breakfast Club's small dining room attracts crowds daily.

and bacon or sausage, or served as a side with biscuits and gravy, starring chorizo gravy and crème fraiche biscuits.

The chef brought a bounty of experience to Saddle Creek, including time at Omaha classics, such as Taxi's and Plank. He worked at The Market House in the Old Market before it was destroyed in a 2016 fire caused by a gas line explosion.

Like a mechanic working his magic on a car in the former gas station, Chef Chase creates delicious masterpieces that celebrate his love for the morning meal.

1540 North Saddle Creek
402-932-5970
facebook.com/SCBCOmaha

CRANE COFFEE

What started as a coffee cart in the old Brandeis Building in downtown Omaha grew into Omaha's "Original Coffeehouse." Espresso Express served coffee in the former department store building for a couple of years until its founder leased a spot along Thirteenth Street, appropriately called 13th Street Coffee.

Created by Steve Hammerstrom, a Seattleite, who moved to Omaha to be with his fiancé, Crane Coffee opened because he missed his Seattle-style coffee—cappuccinos, espressos. He changed the name to Crane Coffee in 1995 because of an affinity for the Sandhill crane, a bird that's made an annual springtime migration through central Nebraska for thousands of years. He thought the name and symbol of the bird perfectly described the area. The company has since been sold to current owner Keith Graeve.

With eight locations scattered around Omaha (the company previously sold the 13th Street Coffee location), it's easy to find a cup of Crane Coffee's smooth-tasting java. Don't expect to find a Crane Coffee location in another city, as the company seeks to keep its brand local. They envision opening more locations around the Metro area. Crane Coffee calls the Cass Street location its first official coffeehouse.

With its bakery and roasting operation at its Sixtieth and Center store, Crane Coffee handles its own distribution process.

7772 Cass Street
402-343-0000
mycranecoffee.com

Top left: TJ Thorson prepares a coffee for a customer.

Top right: The Cass Street location was the first to become Crane Coffee.

Bottom left: Crane Coffee was Omaha's first coffeehouse.

Bottom right: Crane Coffee bakes its pastries at the Sixtieth Street location.

DANTE

Nick Strawhecker knew he was taking a chance when he decided to open a new restaurant during America's Great Recession. Furthermore, he knew that opening a Neapolitan-style pizza restaurant in Omaha may have been a bigger risk, but not only did Dante survive the recession, but the restaurant also became one of the most popular in a city of restaurants. From locally owned to national chains, restaurants seem to be as prevalent in Omaha as Starbucks in Seattle.

But to know how Dante came to be is to know Chef Nick's culinary journey. From a young Omaha boy to a world traveler, the chef's palate was first defined at home, helping his grandmother prepare meals and then polished overseas. His dad worked for First Data, so the family moved often. Living in London, the family traveled around Europe, allowing Nick to sample all types of food from several countries. This also helped develop an early interest in restaurants.

Returning to Omaha, a young Nick wanted to develop his culinary skills, so he attended culinary school in Rhode Island. Later eschewing a bachelor's degree at Northern Arizona University in favor of studying abroad as part of a chef's program, Nick found himself in Italy's Piedmont region, where he would complete a Masters Chef Program before also working with renowned chefs in Tuscany. He later returned to the United States, where he also worked under the tutelage of a James Beard Award-winning chef in Chicago before working in Philadelphia.

The chef returned home in 2008, with plans to open a restaurant. Seeking to find the perfect spot, he decided to open Dante at The Shops of Legacy in West Omaha. Combined with retail shops and other restaurants, the area was on the verge of becoming a popular area of the city. Then the Great Recession hit. Businesses closed, and

Left: Dante brought Neapolitan pizza to Omaha.
Right: Chef Nick Strawhecker. Photo courtesy of Dante.

people lost jobs. Although unsure of the future, Chef Nick believed in his vision and opened Dante in early 2009.

Opening night could have been an omen, as a snowstorm hit Omaha. Traffic was initially slow, but Chef Nick continued to believe in his restaurant. Then customers started to visit and enjoy the food and wine. Word of mouth spread that the food was delicious, and Dante had some of the best wine in Omaha. Since then Dante annually competes as one of the pizzerias in Omaha during citywide contests. Nick opened a second Dante location in the Blackstone District in 2018.

Dante's serves authentic Neapolitan pizza. The restaurant meets international requirements to be considered a Neapolitan pizzeria, including using San Marzano tomatoes (raised near Mount Vesuvius) and specific flour as well as a certain style of mozzarella cheese. The fire-burning oven nears eight hundred degrees, baking pizza in ninety seconds.

While popular for its pizza, Dante also creates superb seasonal-based pasta dishes as well as other entrées. The restaurant strives to use farm-to-table ingredients as much as possible, with dozens of local and regional farms and distributors.

16901 Wright Plaza, Number 173
402-932-3078
dantepizzeria.com

WERNER PARK

"Take me out the ball game. Take me out to the crowd. Buy me some peanuts and cracker jack . . ." offers a new meaning for ballpark cuisine. You used to be able to count on getting a hot dog, peanuts, and cracker jack during a baseball game, but the Omaha Storm Chasers took ballpark food to a whole new level during their games at Werner Park. You can skip the hot dog with sauerkraut and go for a footlong topped with pulled pork or barbecue. Or, perhaps you prefer a footlong Chicago Dawg, with special relish, mustard, onions, and a few hot peppers.

Teams expanded concession menus to help attract fans to baseball games. Minor league teams, such as the Pacific Coast League's Storm Chasers, brainstorm ideas, coming up with such gems as vanilla ice cream sandwiched between fruity pop tarts. Barbecue brisket egg rolls hit a homerun with fans during the 2018 season.

While teams can add specialty one-season items to the choices, popular entrées permanently remain on the menu. Valentino's pizza, a local pizza company, offers a few types of slices during the games. Its menu also includes lasagna, a favorite that tastes as good as what you'd eat at the buffet restaurant. The Werner Park dish is large enough to share between two or three people. La Mesa, a Mexican food chain popular in the area, offers restaurant-quality tacos, burritos, and nachos. You can even ask for your nachos to be made with tater tots instead of tortilla chips. World-famous Omaha Steaks steak burgers are also sold at Werner Park.

If you're a baseball park food traditionalist, don't fret, as hot dogs and bratwursts are available with all the toppings.

Since the Triple-A baseball season runs from early April to Labor Day weekend, the Werner Park menu isn't available year-round.

Top left: Chicken and waffles are popular at the ballpark.

Top right: Fans can order barbecue among the concession stands around Werner Park.

Bottom left: A statue of Hall-of-Famer and local star Bob Gibson greets visitors to Werner Park.

Bottom right: A pop tart ice cream treat was a popular dessert during the 2018 season.

12356 Ballpark Way
402-738-5100
milb.com/omaha

B&B GRILL AND ARCADE

A hot dog joint named after two hot dogs. That's the best way to describe Bellevue's B&B Grill and Arcade. The restaurant's theme is based on the owners' dogs—Birdie and Bogie. From the giant Hot Dog Man greeting diners near the front door to the paw prints to the counter, B&B definitely lets you know the dogs are in charge.

Diane Bruce opened the restaurant in 2013 after being laid off from her job as a defense contractor. She wanted a family-friendly environment for the couple's grandchildren and friends near their Bellevue home instead of having to drive across the Metro for family outings. Add the fact that their hot dogs—with all kinds of toppings—were often the first thing eaten at cookouts and you had the ingredients for B&B.

Originally named B&B Classic Hot Dogs, the company changed its name in late 2018 to B&B Grill and Arcade. The restaurant fielded calls from people wanting to board their dogs for a weekend. Imagine their surprise when the callers found out it was a hot dog restaurant and not a bed and breakfast for dogs.

The menu includes more than twenty hot dogs—quarter- and half-pounders—with such names as Buffalo Bacon Dog (a bacon-wrapped hot dog dipped in Buffalo wing sauce), Cowboy Killa (includes siracha-flavored sour cream), and the Derf, an original hot dog featuring a hickory applewood-smoked hot dog topped with barbecue sauce, onions, and shredded cheese.

While the menu entices the senses, a challenge awaits those brave enough to take on the Dogzilla. Challengers have twenty-five minutes to eat a three-pound hot dog with all the toppings. Many enter the ring, but only a few—seven to be precise—have won the contest to get their picture on the Weiner Whomper Wall of Fame. Losers pay twenty-five dollars for the meal and get their photo on the Weenie Wall of Shame.

Left: The hot dog statue is popular with guests.

Middle top: B&B creates unique hot dog combinations for special events.

Middle: B&B offers a buffet breakfast on Sundays.

Middle bottom: The restaurant offers a variety of hot dog combos.

Right: The wall of honor for successfully eating the Dogzilla.

B&B offers more than hot dogs, though. They have a burger dog, which is an oblong-style hamburger served on a hot dog bun. Additional menu items include sides, such as French fries, baked beans, and coleslaw, as well as salads and chicken sandwiches.

Friday night was steak night, which partner Jerry Charvat started. Following his passing in 2018, the family decided to not continue the event. Instead, B&B continues to use the barbecue rub Jerry created, offering special BBQ items such as ribs and smoked pork chops. A breakfast buffet is available Sunday mornings and includes scrambled eggs alongside the eatery's popular bread pudding dessert.

The restaurant's arcade appeals to "kids of all ages." With classic pinball games and contemporary video contests, an evening at B&B Grill and Arcade provides an entertaining outing for anyone.

1020 Lincoln Road
402-905-9541
bbhotdogs.com

LITTLE KING DELI & SUBS

The culinary world bestowed royalty upon Omaha when Little King opened its first location in 1969. Since then, the restaurant chain has been part of the city's gastronomic landscape, with people just saying "No. 11" when ordering. The Royal Treat, which is No. 11 on the menu, is the most popular sandwich at Little King.

It features ham, hard salami, prosciutto, capicola, and provolone cheese. The "Little King Way" adds lettuce, tomato, onion, salt, and oregano, topped with oil and vinegar on white or wheat bread. The sandwich comes in two sizes—king size (about twelve inches) and regular (six inches). Additional toppings can be added. The restaurant serves a variety of other sandwiches as well as soup, chili, and sides, such as macaroni or potato salad.

From the first restaurant at 80th and Dodge, founder Sid Wertheim grew the Omaha-based restaurant to a national chain with more than a hundred restaurants in seventeen states. After another company bought Little King from Wertheim, the company fell on hard times. After failing to compete nationally, most of the restaurants closed. The Wertheims bought the company back eighteen years later and scaled it down to being an Omaha product.

Bob Wertheim, Sid's son, eventually took over running the company. He expanded locations around Omaha. Today, five Little Kings dot the Omaha landscape, with two more in Lincoln. Wertheim sold the company in 2012. The current owners plan to build another national chain based on the King.

14005 Q Street
402-896-6347
littlekingsubs.com

Top left: You watch your order being prepared in front of you.

Top right: Little King started in Omaha in the late 1960s.

Bottom left: Little King's dining rooms offer a comfortable dining experience.

Bottom right: The Royal Treat is Little King's top selling menu item.

UNION PACIFIC CAFÉ

As president in the early 1860s, Abraham Lincoln prioritized building a transcontinental railroad. Omaha won the political battle to be the launching spot for westward expansion. Today, the nation's largest railroad company calls the city home. Located inside the nineteen-floor downtown skyscraper, the Union Pacific Cafeteria offers upscale-style cuisine at fast-food prices. UP's headquarters, which manages rail operations in twenty-three western states, has been located in one of Omaha's tallest buildings since 2004.

While the cafeteria's culinary team creates dishes worthy of executives, the café is open to the public weekdays. The chef creates dishes featuring such items as grilled salmon, Churrasco-style steak, and housemade potato chips. With five food stations offering a variety of menu items, including burgers and deli sandwiches, the café's taco salad is known to be a hit with locals.

Managed by California-based Guckenheimer Dining Services, the cafeteria primarily supports hundreds of employees who work at the headquarters. Being centrally located, however, the café attracts employees from other companies as well as people who happen to be in the area because of its delicious menu. The cafeteria sponsors pop-up lunches, featuring local chefs creating dishes associated with their restaurants.

1400 Douglas Street
402-544-3663
dining.guckenheimer.com/clients/unionpacific/fss/fss.nsf

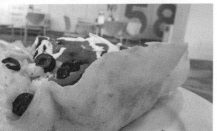

Top left: The café is open to Union Pacific employees, as well as the public.

Bottom left: Taco salad is a popular item on the UP Café menu.

Right: The Union Pacific headquarters is located in downtown Omaha.

Union Pacific Café chefs create their meals from scratch, using fresh, locally sourced items for healthy meal options.

FARMER BROWNS

Call Farmer Browns the Little Steakhouse on the Prairie and you may be right. When it opened in 1964, corn and soybean fields surrounded Waterloo. Today, farm fields still surround the town of about nine hundred. It seems a fitting scene for the steakhouse that attracts visitors from around the world. It's home to some of the best beef in Nebraska and, some say, the country.

Sitting in a nondescript building off the town's main street, you may mistake it for a warehouse, but the Farmer Browns sign above the building stands out. Once inside, sip a drink in the bar or enjoy your meal in the large dining room reminiscent of the 1970s. Farmer Browns' reputation includes outstanding food in a simple, comfortable atmosphere.

Not planning to run a restaurant for decades, Charlie Stenglein bought a then small café after being talked into it by his brother, a real estate agent. With no experience in the food industry, Charlie and wife Daphne turned the restaurant, which they renamed Farmer Browns after a few years, into a popular steakhouse. Charlie learned to properly cut meat from butchers he trusted. The owners sought out the best butcher shops to work with to provide high-quality meat for their customers. He and Daphne ran Farmer Browns along with their sons until Charlie passed away in 1982.

Their son Steve then managed the daily operations with his brother Ben, but now runs Farmer Browns himself. Daphne and her twin sister, Dagmar Luenenburg, took on hosting duties. Customers loved being greeted by the sisters, which many considered the best

On their word of mouth reputation:
"If you don't give them a good quality meal and service, they won't come back."

Top left: Farmer Browns is located near downtown Waterloo.

Top right: Farmer Browns has been popular since its early days.

Bottom left: Artwork in the restaurant.

Bottom right: A porterhouse steak dinner with all the trimmings.

part of visiting Farmer Browns (which says a lot considering how amazing the food tastes). The twins died within a year of each other, with Dagmar passing in 2001 and Daphne in 2002.

Under the sons' guidance, Farmer Browns' reputation grew, including being named one of the best steakhouses in the country by Thrillist and Travel Channel. People who learned about Farmer Browns online have traveled around the world to enjoy a meal there.

As Farmer Browns grew in popularity over the years, the owners expanded the restaurant, nearly doubling it to about eight thousand square feet. With a party room available for celebrations and events, the restaurant can serve large groups while also attending to the needs of other diners.

2620 River Road Drive
402-779-2353
farmerbrowns.com

RUNZA

With its headquarters in Lincoln, Runza owns more than eighty locations, mainly in Nebraska but also in Iowa, Colorado, and Kansas. Especially popular in Omaha, more than twenty locations are in the Metro area.

The first Runza restaurant opened in Lincoln's Pioneer Park area in 1949, when the Everett family decided to share its version of the Eastern European bierock. Their version, which they called a Runza, consists of seasoned ground beef, mixed with cabbage and onions, baked inside a dough pocket. While it's considered fast food, most people who've had one would say it's a step above. Runzas can be customized, or you can order a specialty Runza, such as the Swiss Mushroom, BBQ Bacon, or Cheeseburger.

With the Runza sandwich its original menu item, the restaurant also offers other specialties, including fresh, handmade burgers. Some diners struggle choosing between the two. Runza is also famous for its frings, hand-battered onion rings mixed with crinkle-cut French fries.

During cooler weather, Runza offers a Nebraska favorite, a bowl of homemade chili with a side of cinnamon rolls, a staple of Nebraska elementary schools.

5051 Center Street
402-556-2540
runza.com

"I've be[...] the USA
and Nebraska 2 times.
I could eat Runza®
3 times a day!"
Bernard - Kikongooni, Kenya

Top left: Inside Millard's Runza.

Top right: Runza has more than eighty locations, mostly in Nebraska.

Bottom left: A Nebraska favorite—Runza with frings and chili.

Bottom right: Runza has an international appeal.

Cinnamon Rolls and Chili together? Yes, it's a thing. Make sure to try Runza's homemade Chili with a cinnamon roll drizzled with icing. It's so popular, it's a combo meal option on the menu.

B&G TASTY FOODS

Iowa claims to be the home of "loose meat" sandwiches, but B&G Tasty Foods gives any Iowan a run for their money. Supposedly created in Iowa during the 1920s, loose meat sandwiches consist of ground beef mixed with onions and some salt topped on a hamburger bun. Think Sloppy Joe's without the sloppy.

Opened as a drive-in at Eightieth and Dodge streets in 1953—the outskirts of Omaha at the time—B&G Tasty Food has enjoyed being part of the Omaha food scene for more than sixty-five years. The drive-in was a basic operation. Customers ordered their loose meat sandwich and French fries at the window, and a carhop would deliver the food to their car. The drive-in closed in 1973 and moved to Beverly . . . Beverly Hills Plaza, that is (a little *Beverly Hillbillies* humor).

The owners maintained a stake in the business until 2000, when one of their daughters took over. The current owner, Eddie Morin, actually started working at the restaurant in 2001 while in high school and eventually bought it in 2009. Eddie has run it since then as his life's love.

Keeping the recipes as they have been since the 1950s, Eddie believes in maintaining B&G Tasty's core menu. They've added such items as Frenchees (a fried cheese sandwich) and salads, but the menu mainly remains true to its opening day.

"The recipes are the same as in '53," Eddie says. "The chili is the same. Shakes are one of the mainstays."

B&G Tasty Foods knows it's a fast-food restaurant, though some customers think of it as a diner. Eddie expanded the restaurant in 2011, adding a party room, which allows large groups, such as birthday celebrations, to dine together.

Diners enjoy a nostalgic visit along with their meal, as the restaurant features pictures and posters reflecting on B&G Tasty

Top left: Loose meat sandwiches, chili, and fries are popular.

Right: Pictures of the first location are displayed at the Dodge Street location.

Bottom left: B&G eclectic décor includes old bikes and photos.

Foods' history. From pictures of the original drive-in to menu boards from 1953 and 1973, Eddie wants diners to enjoy a fun experience. Bicycles, including vintage Stingrays, hang from the wall above the booths.

Enjoy your Bee Gee sandwich—that's the name for the loose meat treat—at the counter, which dates back to a 1926 Ben Franklin store.

Just like 1953, you need to top off your meal with a root beer float for dessert.

7900 West Dodge Road
402-390-6096
bgtastyfoods.com

LEO'S DINER

In the Benson neighborhood, it's likely you'll see a hipster with a knit beanie atop his head sitting at the counter next to a retired person wearing a John Deere cap. You might think they'd have nothing to talk about other than the weather, but at Leo's Diner, everyone comes across as friends. A part of Benson for more than sixty-five years, Leo's has seen several changes through the years, but in the end, everyone looks for a quality breakfast and lunch.

While Benson underwent a transition from an aging section of Omaha, adding art galleries, chic retro stores, and a score of contemporary-style restaurants and bars, Leo's continued to operate as a local diner, providing much of the same menu as it has for decades. From corned beef hash and eggs to biscuits and gravy, comfort food dominates the menu.

Wanting to keep the restaurant's flavor, Jason and Emily Brown kept the restaurant's décor the same for several years after purchasing it in 2004. A 2018 renovation strived to maintain a 1960s décor while adding new booths and flooring. Black-and-white photos of the Benson area hang on the brick wall. A classic '60s counter invites people to sit on the barstools and travel back in time as they enjoy their meal.

Telling her mother one day that she and Jason were interested in buying a restaurant, Emily learned that Leo's was available. Taking over the diner proved personal for Emily, as her father, a longtime Union Pacific employee, frequented Leo's.

A fun part of owning Leo's Diner is the customers, Emily says. She recalls a younger customer standing up at the counter one morning and belting out a song. Obviously feeling the effects of partying too much the night before, some people joined him in song, while others watched and applauded afterward. It was then that she realized what a great community Leo's was a part of.

Top left: Owners sought to keep Leo's nostalgic feel during a renovation.

Middle left: Breakfast at Leo's Diner is a walk down memory lane.

Bottom left: Leo's Diner remains a Benson staple as the neighborhood transitions to an art and music district.

Right: Some booths still have jukeboxes.

6055 Maple Street
402-553-2280
facebook.com/leosdinerbenson

RESTAURANTS A-Z

Alpine Inn, 38
10405 Calhoun Road

Amato's Café and Catering, 2
6405 Center Street

B&B Grill and Arcade, 192
1020 Lincoln Road

B&G Tasty Foods, 202
7900 West Dodge Road

Big Mama's Kitchen, 178
3223 North 45th Street

Block 16, 132
1611 Farnam Street

Bronco's, 62
1123 South 120th Street

Brother Sebastian's Steak
House and Winery, 46
1350 South 119th Street

California Tacos and More, 160
3235 California Street

Catfish Lake, 78
1006 Cunningham Road

Coneflower Creamery, 60
3921 Farnam Street

Crane Coffee, 186
7772 Cass Street

Crescent Moon Ale House, 166
3578 Farnam Street

Cupcake Island, 116
1314 South 119th Street

Dairy Twist, 22
2211 Lincoln Road

Dante, 188
16901 Wright Plaza, Number 173

Dinker's Bar and Grill, 112
2368 South 29th Street

The Drover, 138
2121 South 73rd Street

Dundee Dell, 176
5007 Underwood Avenue

eCreamery Ice Cream
& Gelato, 24
5001 Underwood Avenue

Ethnic Sandwich Shop, 6
1438 South 13th Street

Farmer Browns, 198
2620 River Road Drive

Fat Shack BBQ, 34
7440 North 30th Street

Finicky Frank's, 124
9520 Calhoun Road

Flagship Commons, 130
10000 California Street

Gerda's German Restaurant
and Bakery, 30
5180 Leavenworth Street

Godfather's Pizza, 76
3141 North 108th Street

Greek Islands, 44
3821 Center Street

The Grey Plume, 146
220 South 31st Avenue, #3101

Hardy Coffee, 68
2112 North 30th Street

Harold's Koffee House, 20
8327 North 30th Street

Jack and Mary's Restaurant, 52
655 North 114th Street

Jacobo's Authentic Mexican
Grocery and Tortilleria, 82
4621 South 24th Street

The Jaipur, 106
10922 Elm Street

j. coco, 8
5203 Leavenworth Street

Jim and Jennie's Greek
Village, 72
3026 North 90th Street

Joe Tess Place, 54
5424 South 24th Street

John's Grecian Delight, 16
1001 Fort Crook Road North,
Suite 110

Jones Bros. Cupcakes, 36
2121 South 67th Street

Junior's Forgot Store
Bar & Grill, 170
11909 Calhoun Road

Kitchen Table, 118
1415 Farnam Street

La Casa Pizzaria, 182
4432 Leavenworth Street

Le Bouillon, 122
1017 Howard Street

Leo's Diner, 204
6055 Maple Street

Le Voltaire Restaurant and
Le Petit Bakery, 174
569 North 155th Plaza

Lil Burro, 64
12510 South 29th Avenue

Lisa's Radial Café, 134
817 North 40th Street

Lithuanian Bakery, 74
5217 South 33rd Avenue

Little King Deli & Subs, 194
14005 Q Street

Lo Sole Mio, 148
3001 South 32nd Avenue

Louie M's Burger Lust, 12
1718 Vinton Street

Malara's Italian Restaurant, 4
2123 Pierce Street

Metro Community College
Sage Student Bistro, 32
5730 North 30th Street

Modern Love, 10
3157 Farnam Street, Suite 7113

M's Pub, 152
422 South 11th Street

OJ's Café, 162
9201 North 30th Street

Omaha Culinary Tours, 126
omahaculinarytours.com

Omaha Steaks
International, 168
10909 John Galt Boulevard

Orsi's Italian Bakery
and Pizzeria, 28
621 Pacific Street

Over Easy, 150
16859 Q Street

Pepperjax, 66
2429 South 132nd Street

Petrow's, 56
5914 Center Street

Pink Poodle Restaurant, 128
633 Old Lincoln Highway

Ray's Original Buffalo Wings, 26
120 South 31st Avenue,
    Suite 5103

Romeo's Mexican Food
    and Pizza, 180
2395 No. 90th Street

Round the Bend
    Steakhouse, 120
30801 East Park Highway,
    Ashland

Runza, 200
5051 Center Street

Saddle Creek Breakfast
    Club, 184
1540 North Saddle Creek

Saigon Bowl, 154
6307 Center Street

Saigon Restaurant, 154
12100 West Center Road

Saigon Surface, 154
324 South 14th Street

Sakura Bana, 102
7425 Dodge Street

Shirley's Diner, 14
13838 R Plaza

Sinful Burger Sports Grill, 108
4005 Twin Creek Drive

Stella's, 156
106 South Galvin Road

Stoysich House of Sausage, 80
2532 South 24th Street

Surfside Club, 18
14445 North River Drive

Taqueria el Rey, 158
5201 South 24th Street

Taste of Omaha, 172
7015 Spring Street

Ted and Wally's, 144
1120 Jackson Street

Time Out Chicken, 70
3518 North 30th Street

Trini's Mexican Restaurant, 164
1020 Howard Street

Union Pacific Café, 196
1400 Douglas Street

Upstream Brewing
    Company, 110
514 South 11 Street

Vala's Pumpkin Patch, 114
12102 South 180th Street

V. Mertz, 104
1022 Howard Street

Werner Park, 190
12356 Ballpark Way

Whisk + Measure, 58
2505 South 133rd Plaza

Wilson & Washburn, 48
1407 Harney Street

Zio's Pizzeria, 136
7834 Dodge Street

APPENDIX